P9-AQT-668

Women Christian:

New Vision

Mary T. Malone

Religious Education Division
Wm. C. Brown Company Publishers
Dubuque, Iowa

Scripture quotations are from the *Revised Standard Version*, copyright © 1972 by Thomas Nelson, Inc.

Contents

Contents

Preface

This is a book for the nonspecialist. It attempts to bridge the gap between the lecture hall and the daily round, between the feminist theologian and the parish-based Christian woman.

Such a wealth of writing has been appearing over the past few years on the topic of women in the Church that even the committed feminist theologian keeps up to date with difficulty. Studies in exegesis, history, anthropology, biography, spirituality, theology, pour off the presses unceasingly and from all corners of the world. There is a danger that women parishioners will be left behind in this wonderful profusion of material. This book takes a small step towards bridging this information gap.

It is written in the confident knowledge that the main resource for feminists and for the Church is to be found not in books but in the lives of people, and for our purposes, particularly in the lives of women. This is an article of faith in every feminist creed. My hope is that this book will serve as an introduction to feminist theology in two ways. First, it gives a wide sampling of insights from a broad range of feminist writers, and hopefully, it will encourage many women to go directly to these works. I trust that I have not done any of them an injustice in the way I have quoted from them or remembered them from many a reading.

Second, the book is intended to point women towards their own lives, towards a new valuing of their experience, towards a new effort to be faithful to their own original insights, towards a new claiming of their own voice and their own language in the councils of the Churches. No one can speak for all women. The more numerous the voices, the more faithful will our witness be.

Let us join the chorus.

Chapter 1

In God's Own Image

On September 10, 1941, Pope Pius XII addressed a group of newly married couples and spoke in particular to the young women in these words: "Do not be content merely to accept, and— one might say—to tolerate this authority of your husband, to whom God has subjected you according to the dispositions of nature and grace; in your sincere submission you must love that authority. . . ." A little later in the same address, the Pope said: "Many voices will suggest rather a proud autonomy; they will repeat that you are in every respect the equal of your husband, and in many respects his superior. Do not react like Eve to these lying, tempting, deceitful voices."[1]

On October 3, 1983, the archbishop of Quebec, Most Reverend Louis-Albert Vachon, who is also Primate of Canada, spoke as follows, also in Rome: "In our society and in our Church, man has come to think of himself as the sole possessor of rationality, authority, and active initiative, relegating women to the private sector and dependent tasks. Our recognition as Church of our own cultural deformation will allow us to overcome the archaic concepts of womanhood which have been inculcated in us for centuries."[2]

And finally, on July 2, 1984, the *Toronto Star* reports that Catholic women who favor ordination for women are "threatening to withhold their dollars from collection plates to force the Church to take notice." The report suggests that this is one form

1

of "creative protest" which will be taken by the women in order to press towards "full membership in the Roman Catholic Church for women."[3]

These three quotations are like vignettes from a battle front. They document a long and arduous journey for women, for bishops, for Popes, and for the whole Church. It is part of the very nature of this journey that the response of the women of 1941 to the Pope's words was neither invited nor recorded. Respectful silence and acceptance of their lot in life was all that was expected. As we shall see later, we have some clues to the thoughts of their hearts. There is no doubt, however, about the response of the women of 1984. Despite the willingness of the Canadian bishops to acknowledge an ecclesiastical and cultural culpability, the women of North America in 1984 are looking for more than acknowledgments.

Here in three brief quotations is contained a bird's eye view of the history of Christian sexism and Christian feminism. Part of the task of this book will be to attempt to document this history and its implications. A vast literature has grown around this subject with contributions from all over the world. Our task here will be to explore in particular the implications of feminism for the local Church and for parish life.

Feminism, in general, has not had a good press. In its early days it was presumed to be a haven for man-hating females. Years of ridicule and trivialization followed, best exemplified, perhaps, in the persistent mockery of the language issue accompanied by "clever" coinages such as "person holes" (manholes) and "personipulation" (manipulation). Now the press gleefully reports a backlash with "real" women and "real" men reclaiming their rightful place in the sun. All the while the "real" issues have been glaringly and often unknowingly reported elsewhere—in crime statistics, elected officials guffawing about statistics on wife-battering, electioneering promises to women, and news of the world presented as a man's world with occasional peripheral columns on women's issues.[4]

Within the Christian context, the reception has been similar. Despite a vast scholarly output of Christian feminist literature, the issues do not seem to be taken seriously. One author speaks of "bitchy, brittle feminists."[5] One cardinal refers to all this literature as "weightless."[6] One Pope cautions American bishops to

2

give proof of their pastoral ability and leadership "by withdrawing all support from individuals or groups who, in the name of progress, justice or compassion, or for any other reason, promote the ordination of women to the priesthood."[7] By and large, the affairs of the Church continue without much attention to that group which forms more than half of the membership—women. Nevertheless, there are signs that the outlook is not all bleak, signs that feminist issues are beginning to make an impact. And if this were not so, the future of humanity would be dim, for feminism is about humanity, the full humanity of women. It is about experiencing this humanity, promoting it, reflecting on it, acting it out, removing obstacles to its full implementation, and by implication, finding ways to extend the fullness of humanity to all those deprived of it for whatever specious reasons.

Everywhere the Church gathers, women are in the majority—for worship, for education of the next generation in the faith, for volunteer activities and ministry in the parish. Everywhere, that is, except where the Church gathers to make decisions about the lives of women; there they are almost completely absent, and disappear totally at the upper levels of decision making. As the *Toronto Star* article shows, however, there are rumblings in the house of God. The voices of women are being heard, sometimes in anger, but also in love. The angry voices are often the voices of women who are fully in love with the Church, who intend to remain there, and who wish to take their place fully and responsibly among its membership.

This book will attempt to approach Christian feminism from two sides—from the perspective of feminist scholars, theologians, exegetes and historians, and from the perspective of the Roman Catholic woman living her life and faith in the local parish community. It will be an atttempt to build bridges between Christian feminists and Christian women who do not choose to call themselves feminist but whose hopes and dreams are similar, though often unspoken. This will be an attempt to explore hopes held in common, to interpret, to speak both languages.

First, it will be important to clear some ground and describe some approaches to Christian feminism. The words themselves and the issues arouse deep emotions in people both in and out of the Church. My description will be from within the reality of the Roman Catholic Church, even though I am not unaware of the situation in other churches. The word *feminism* and the reality of "feminism" corresponds to many differing experiences and points of view within the Roman Catholic community. Here I choose three ways of describing these experiences and hope in this way to include a large segment of the Catholic Church in North America.[8]

Complementarity

Most Roman Catholic writings by and about women in the forty years since the address of Pope Pius XII seem to have adopted the approach of complementarity. The main tenets of this approach would include the following:

• Women have unique gifts to bring to the Christian community. These gifts have not been fully integrated into Church life and structures in the past. It is now time that this situation be rectified, and that steps be taken to open doors to women gradually. The whole Church will benefit from their gifts used for the good of the Church.

• The gifts are usually presumed to be widely recognized and accepted as "womanly" or "feminine." They usually include gracefulness, gentleness, peacemaking, greater understanding of children, more talent in all aspects of human relationships, and even, as stated in a recent papal document, "a greater natural flair for ministry."[9] These *gifts* are seen to be all the more welcome in that they will counteract the more abrasive "masculine" attributes of present leadership. It is a very traditional approach, going back to the fourth century where separate lists of virtues for women and men were formulated.

• The beauty of women, their motherly qualities, their generosity, patience, and ability to "wait for what they want" are often spoken of in this approach, sometimes in highly emotional language. A quotation from one of the many addresses of Pope Paul VI on the subject will illustrate the point: "You women have always had as your lot the protection of the home, the love of beginnings, and an understanding of cradles. You are present in the mystery of a life beginning. You offer consolation in the departure of death. Our technology runs the risk of becoming inhuman. Reconcile men with life and above all, we beseech you,

4

watch carefully over the future of the race. Hold back the hand of man who, in a moment of folly, might attempt to destroy human civilization."[10]

• The gifts of women are identified in this approach as belonging to her *special nature*, and this is identified specifically in another place by Paul VI as "woman's vocation to be mother." Much will be said later about the "special nature" of women, but suffice it to add here that the reality or supposed reality of woman's "special nature" is foundational to all official teaching about women.

• The gifts or ministries of women in this approach are seen to be auxiliary or secondary to the gifts and ministries of men in the Church. In general, they can be reduced to three; nurturing, being beautiful, and serving. Leadership of any kind, then, is automatically excluded.

One of the characteristics of this approach to feminism is that no critique of the present structures of the Church is included. Even when the Pope fears that men may destroy the world, there is no challenge to men to convert or transform their lives. It is presumed that for better or worse—in this case very much worse— that is the way men are, and that is the way women are. The sins of men, then, become an added burden for women instead of an occasion of repentance for men.

Neither is there a critique of present Church ministerial structures which are open only to men. These structures are seen to be static and given and unchangeable. The integration of the special gifts of women in an auxiliary way may humanize the ministry, but the ministry itself is not perceived to be in need of radical change.

Despite the beautiful and emotional language, women are left with the feeling that there is little room in their spiritual lives for initiative. Their role in the Church is described under what is allowed or permitted or experimental.[11] As many women have discovered, this approach to the role of women in the Church is fragmented at best, and often the cause of frustration and disappointment. At the local level, the inclusion of the gifts of women in the ministry of the Church does not depend on these gifts, but on the willingness of the local pastor to recognize them.

Nevertheless, it should be added that, even while this approach seems to be normative in most parish situations, it has opened the way for countless numbers of women to experience ministry in the Church as ministers of the Eucharist, liturgical readers, hospital visitors, prayer leaders, parish staff members, catechists, catechumenate coordinators, social justice animators and activists, and a whole host of other ministries limited only by the inventiveness and needs of the local community. As we shall see later, this opportunity for ministry in concrete and recognized roles is essential to the renewal of ministry in the Roman Catholic Church. For how can women reflect on their ministry if they have never ministered in a recognized and recognizable way? While there are many half-truths in this "complementarity" approach to the nature and roles of women in the Church, nevertheless, it has been the occasion of renewed hope and reawakened Christian consciousness for thousands of women in many parts of the world. This has created a situation that is, in many ways, irreversible. Doors, once opened, can with great difficulty be closed again. However, as many women have experienced, it only takes a change of pastors in a parish to alter radically the extent to which the gifts of women are recognized and affirmed.

Before this approach is left, it is necessary to add that this attitude towards women corresponds in many respects to prevailing cultural and social attitudes. Women are presented in a thousand ways with a picture of the "formula female,"[12] which is designed, "formulated" in order to beautify and service the world of men. The cultural roles assigned to the formula female are to be sex object and servant to males. Young girls are socialized into this role, and from a very early age learn to experience life at second hand. Each generation of males defines the expected kind of beauty and the expected forms of service, but the underlying principle remains the same. And it corresponds closely with the "special nature" traditional in Christian writing about women. Women are not quite possessed of human nature. They have a *special* nature, and so a billion dollar advice industry is seen to be imperative to help women fulfill their allotted destinies. The range of advice is vast—from cosmetics to marriage, from health to wealth, from hygiene to holidays. The greater part of this book will be taken up with the exploration of the consequences of this approach to women which sees them as complementary to men. Enough has been said here to sketch the rough outlines of the issues involved.

Post-Christian Feminism

The women included in this second approach are the women most frequently subjected to public critique and often ridicule. As the name implies, these are the women whose frustration with Church structures and ecclesiastical dicta about "auxiliary ministries" and "special natures" finally led them to make a break with their Christian heritage in a conscious and definitive way. For many women, this included leaving the Church of their childhood devotion and adult commitment, often with so much anger that reconciliation seemed forever impossible. These women saw through the flaws of the "complementarity" approach; often they had experienced hiring and firing and rehiring and retiring. Often, too, decades of commitment and ministry within the Church were cut off at the whim of some local leadership. As will be immediately obvious, anger is a dominant characteristic. While many women have left the Church because of its intransigence on the role of women, many others share the anger but still remain. Often they wonder how much more they can tolerate, but the love and commitments of a lifetime prevent them from forsaking a Church which causes more pain than joy, more frustration than hope.

Whenever a group of Roman Catholics gather, some of these women can be found. In general, their anger and grief does not find a sympathetic ear from their sisters or from their brothers in the faith. Parish communities are ill-equipped generally to deal with anger, frustration, and breaking relationships whether in the human or faith dimensions. This is the reason why so many women in such situations seek support elsewhere, with other women, other groups. Women's groups spring up wherever "two or three are gathered" and often indeed discover that even in their rage Jesus is among them.

A great deal of profoundly important writing and research has originated from such groups. It is from their shared experience that feminist reflection and analysis stems. It is this shared experience that gives rise to a new way of doing theology, a new

7

way of reading our history and our traditions. Often enough this historical and theological and biblical exploration leads to such depths of anger and trauma that no hope of ever receiving strength and life from the Christian tradition is envisaged. Many women have begun to explore other feminist traditions, such as matriarchy and witchcraft. Many women simply abandon the whole enterprise and seek to heal their broken lives and dreams whatever way they can.[13]

This is a rage that few men can understand. It includes anger at oneself for living or existing for so long with a false consciousness, for living life at second hand, for rationalizing a supposed inferiority into a virtue. It is traumatic to discover that one's identity is based on a lie, and many women do not discover within themselves or within society the support and resources to refocus their lives. The history of insanity charts many such stories. Theology and psychiatry have often assured women that if they cannot accept things as they are, they must be sick or sinful.

Many of us know such women. Many of us have experienced this anger ourselves. Many of us have watched with confusion, fear, and sometimes ridicule as a close friend, colleague, or relative has gone through such a crisis. Let us learn to listen, to respect the source and cause of such anger. Let us learn not to judge. Let us build the kinds of communities in which it will not be necessary to lose any more genuine gifts of women from the Church.

Critical Theology of Liberation

This third approach has been so named by Elizabeth Schussler Fiorenza, although it is quite possible to be numbered here without ever having heard of a critical theology of liberation.[14] Women in this group are women who are learning to claim their history—a wounded, fragmented, repressed, untold story—as their own as Christian, and as integral to the Church. The three words of the heading may need some explanation.

• *Critical* refers to this moment in history which is being experienced by women Christians as a critical moment, a moment of crisis. Times of crisis call for action and decision, for conversion and renewal, for leaving the old and safe behind and moving toward the unknown.

8

• *Theology* refers to the kind of reflection that takes place in the moment of crisis, a reflection which opens new doors of understanding to the divine and human. It is a theology shaped in both the experience of trauma and the hope for a new future. It is a theology that calls us to live in "anticipatory obedience" to that future. It is a clear-eyed theology, awakened to the attitudes that must be denounced, the repression that must be prevented, and also to the power of the Spirit moving in the hearts of women and men to create a new future for the Church, a community of equal disciples.

• *Liberation* refers to the fundamental humanizing claim of the gospel of Jesus Christ to lead people from slavery to freedom. It refers here especially to the liberation of women, but is alert to the fact that, unless all are liberated, no one is liberated. And so, women in this group feel an instinctive and also a deliberately sought alliance with all people everywhere who are working for the liberation of human beings.

Women and men in this group are committed to a long journey and a heavy task. The Christian task, from its foundational documents to its most recent experience, from its smallest parish to its most universal dimension, has to be reclaimed through the eyes of women. Women in the Church have no history except as marginalized. This history must be reclaimed, not to excuse or explain away, or to be rationalized, but reclaimed precisely as a wounded history. The pain of generations of women must be told. The glories of generations of women must be told. Women of today must be able to feel solidarity with the women who have gone before us, so that their Church becomes ours, and our story becomes the Church's story. Women know well that it is not the only story but it is the story of more than half of the Church's membership, and it has never been told.

In a word, it is the story of women under patriarchy,[15] of women who were considered of no account in the generations of the Church's life when, as Archbishop Vachon suggested, men came to think of themselves as the sole possessor of rationality, authority, and active initiative, "relegating women to the private sector and dependent tasks."

It is the story of women whose spiritual lives were accounted of no value to the Church; of women who were never consulted

9

about the decisions which affected their lives; of women whose sanctity was expressed in a language which spoke of sonship and brotherhood; of women who with great difficulty, if at all, internalized the experience of Godlikeness or Christlikeness or Spiritedness because the only way of describing these experiences was in a language designed only for male experience and male realities. It is a story of women today, who having experienced the same realities, now seek signs of liberation in our own spiritual lives, our own ministries, our own history, our own sources, and our own bodies.

These women do not seek integration into sexist structures, even while they try to live out their spiritual and ecclesial lives in a Church marked in almost every aspect by the sins of patriarchal sexism. Neither do these women seek utopian withdrawal from the Church or the world of men, for they know that in such withdrawal lies ultimate despair. These women look for the transformation of women **and** men **and** the Church. They are no longer content to hold back the hands of men from their own and others' destruction. Rather they challenge men and women within and without the Church to accept the challenge of humanity. These women seek empowerment of themselves and their sisters in the faith. They seek empowerment of all women everywhere. For the first time in thousands of years of Church history, women are claiming the right and privilege of defining themselves as a matter of justice, based on the liberating gospel of Jesus Christ.

Such then are three possible ways of looking at Christian feminism. They include women and men in various stages of consciousness, and, with varying degrees of commitment, to the Christian community. They include women who have experienced no discomfort with their roles as Christian women, and women who have been so distraught at the discovery of the Church's history of sexism, that they found themselves unable to continue to identify themselves as Christian. They also include women whose very hope comes from the pain and disappointment that they have experienced, because in this pain they feel solidarity with women at every age in the history of the Church, and from this renewed sense of solidarity, new hope arises.

And these ways include men who often ask with bewilderment: "What exactly do these women want?" They include men who know very well what women want and are determined that

10

they will not attain their goals. They include men who have set out to hear and listen and accompany women on their journey, who know how to lend their support but not their advice, who share their knowledge but not their prejudices.

Before this first chapter is completed, it will be helpful to outline briefly, as a kind of aperitif, the issues that will be raised again and again in the course of this book. As women begin to experience their empowerment at the heart of the Church, or more correctly, as women begin to claim this empowerment, hardly one item on the Christian agenda remains untouched. Here we wish to highlight fourteen issues which will reclaim our attention repeatedly.

1. Personhood. If women were defined as having a "special nature," males were defined as being normatively human. This distorted understanding of personhood appears to be at the basis of most official Church teaching about humanity. Often persons are said to come equally from the hand of God and to have an equal destiny in the hereafter. Here below, however, such equality does not exist. As women claim their full humanity, the original sin of distorted humanity will have to be confessed, repented of, and forgiven.

2. Relationships. It follows from the above that the structures of human relationships were and are similarly flawed. Patriarchal structures do not make for equal partnerships. As Pius XII pointed out, there is room for only one will, that of the male.[16] We know from our own families that such a structure was capable of producing loving relationships; but few among us are unaware of the anguish and broken dreams that were also integral to such relationship structures.

3. God. Humans were made in "God's own image," but few women ever heard the feminine side of that image integrated into the worship life of the Church. Precisely the contrary was true. Sometimes blatantly, sometimes in sophisticated theological language, the ability of women to image of God was denied. As women learn to discover the depths of their own spiritual experience, the imaging of God will change. Perhaps it is here that the most profound consequences of Christian feminism resided. How do we begin to speak of a God who is imaged in the female as in

11

the male, and who is most fully imaged in the equal discipleship of women and men together?

4. Church. "As for us, let us recognize the ravages of sexism, and our own male appropriation of Church institutions and numerous aspects of the Christian life. Need I mention the example of the masculine language of our official—and even liturgical—texts?" So spoke Archibishop Vachon at the Synod on Reconciliation.[17] It is easy to see the necessary changes in the life and structures of the Church if men are not only to recognize but also to heal these unjust situations. In fact, the archbishop implied that the future of the Church depends on such a recognition. For, he said, how can the Church demand justice from others "unless the recognition of women as full members becomes, simultaneously, a reality within the Church itself?" A further indication of the present injustice to women in church structures is the use of the expression *full members* as a future reality for women in the Church.

5. Theology. Women, and all other oppressed peoples, have discovered or rediscovered a new way of theologizing. Traditional theology has theoretically been conducted in an atmosphere of high neutrality and profound objectivity. Feminist theologians, among others, have helped us to see how many vested interests were supported by a supposedly objective theology. Ivory-tower theology is not, therefore, free of prejudice. Women have learned to theologize from the midst of their struggle for acceptance in the Church. They lay no claims to objectivity. It is a highly committed theology, committed to the humanization of women and the whole race. At the moment the signs are only dimly apparent, but the future of theological education and the whole theological enterprise is faced with one of the most profound changes in direction since the Pauline mission.

6. Scriptures. Any woman who has ever been addressed as "my brother" during the Liturgy of the Word, will be forgiven for thinking that the Good News is addressed only to the males of the congregation. The next few chapters will explore the Scriptures, but we can remark here that the Scriptures until very recently have been interpreted and preached only by men. Even on a human level, this is bound to produce a one-sided view. On a literary level, it has meant that stories of women have been suppressed, omitted, or reinterpreted. On a faith level, it means that the rich and diverse testimony to the lives of women in the Scriptures has been forgotten. A rereading of the Scriptures by women is already enriching the Church with new insights, and new facts about our origins as a Christian community.

7. World. For centuries, the home has been seen as woman's domain. Involvement with the "world" was reserved for men. Only within recent memory have circumstances changed. Women have won the vote and now politicians are falling over each other trying to lure the voting power of women. When elections loom on the horizon in both the United States and Canada, the women's vote is understood to make all the difference between victory and defeat. This enormous social and cultural change has not been without its toll on the lives of women and men and families. As women take their rightful place on the world scene, the world is shrinking to the dimensions of a global village. The Church's stance before the world changed radically at the Second Vatican Council.[18] Now the implications of those changes face us all.

8. Leadership. Most girls are socialized to expect to follow. Most boys are socialized to expect to lead. Past generations summed up the role of women in such aphorisms as "The hand that rocks the cradle rules the world." The leadership of women was hidden, vicarious, devious, manipulative. So the mythology went. There was one model of leadership and it had been designed by men for men. As women move into leadership positions on all fronts (except, of course, the Roman Catholic Church), new models of leadership are being discovered. Women have discovered that leadership does not need to be hierarchical; it does not need to be competitive; it need not be based on the principle that some win, but most lose. Women are discovering that there are leadership models which allow all to win. Women are discovering that such leadership models are recommended in the Gospels as being characteristic of the life of Christians.

9. Spiritual life. How do women with "special natures" who are not fully human, and not fully members of the Church pray to a God who is always imaged in male terms and worshipped in male-led liturgies? The answer is apparent in the difficulty shown by women speaking of their spiritual lives. No wonder, since *spiritual* was defined as the opposite of what women were. Women represented the carnal, men the spiritual. This most secret dimension of a woman's relationship with her God is being expressed more in song, in art, in poetry, in life, in dance than in word. But the spiritual lives of women are being renewed. Broken images are being reconstructed. New symbols are being discovered. The secret core of a woman's life, hitherto alienated as *sinful* is being reclaimed as *holy*. When, in the course of time, this vast new resource will be shared fully with the Church, a new creation will come into being.

10. Justice. Over the past few years, the Church has been characterized before the world as the guardian and spokesperson of justice for the poor and afflicted and exploited of the world. Women in the Church have been officially and explicitly excluded from this concern. In official Church terms, the women's issue is not a justice issue. Women, however, know otherwise. Many women, in fact, claim that the fundamental justice issue is the oppression of women, one half of the human race. All people who work actively for justice on any front know that all the justice issues are intertwined. If there is not justice for all, there is justice for none. As has been shown, the Canadian bishops have acknowledged that unless there is justice within the Church itself, their demands for justice elsewhere will ring hollow.

11. Language. New experiences demand a new language. Here is another task facing feminists, and it is a particularly grievous one for Christian feminists. Whenever the Church gathers to pray, it is through the mediation of males praying in male formulae to God who is always imaged as male. This is one of the emotional frontiers over which many local battles are fought. Most current solutions range from ridicule to outright refusal to change a fixed language. There are few attentive and sympathetic voices raised within the ranks of the ordained clergy. Even here, however, there are some creative solutions—while we await justice. We shall examine some of these later.

12. Ministry. Ministry in the Roman Catholic Church generally means the "ordained" ministry. Even when "lay" ministry is included, its meaning and implementation are defined and enacted by the ordained. The service of lay people, in practice, becomes ministry when it is recognized as such by the local ordained leader. As shall be shown, this is not the biblical meaning of ministry, nor the original Christian practice of ministry.

13. Education. Theological education is changing. The halls of learning are now being trod by women. Graduation ceremonies for most men include ordination; for Roman Catholic women, they often include the unemployment line. Not perhaps since the catechetical school of Alexandria in the time of Origen has theological education been so readily available to women. *Readily* in the preceding sentence does not mean without cost and without sacrifice. But more and more women are ready and willing and are entering ecclesiastical institutions. There they receive the same theological education as their brothers who then proceed to ordination with no further qualification except their maleness. The influence of these women is being felt not only in their final ministerial situation, should they find one, but also in the theological education their presence is causing to be redefined.

14. Sex. Nun, witch, playmate, whore, goddess, wife—whatever the list used, the role of a woman was defined by the way she used or abstained from sex.[19] Every statement in the Christian tradition in the last several decades connected sex for women with motherhood. When women are seen as equal partners in a sexual relationship, when the violence of men can be distinguished from their "right" to sex with any available female, a profound revolution in human mores will be under way. A woman's sexuality is under formation from the first moment of her existence. Most women have begun the task of unlearning the negative input which, in almost every culture and every home, led them to see themselves as sex objects. In this area, perhaps, is the task of liberation most delicate.

Such then is one glimpse of the vast canvas that is needed to paint a true picture of Christian feminism. When women claim their blessed right to image God equally with males, a new creation is aborning among us. The canvas is so vast that no one book can do more than touch up some of the colors. This is the task at hand.

Chapter 2

And There Was a Woman

> *Now he was teaching in one of the synagogues on the sab-*
> *bath. And there was a woman who had a spirit of infirmity for*
> *eighteen years; she was bent over and could not fully straighten*
> *herself. And when Jesus saw her, he called her and said to her,*
> *"Woman, you are freed from your infirmity." And he laid his*
> *hands upon her, and immediately she was made straight, and*
> *she praised God. (Luke 13:10–13)*

In the preceding chapter, three approaches to the question of women in the Church were outlined. The remainder of this book will be written specifically from the perspective of the third approach—a critical theology of liberation. More simply, this means that the remainder of the book will be a reflection by a woman who has chosen to remain within the Church, conscious of a new belonging, and empowered by new insights and gifts from so many sisters who have made a similar choice.[1] The New Testament is the touchstone of the Christian faith, and so our journey begins there. This is one area where a great amount of scholarly work has already been done by women and my debt to them is obvious.[2] From all of this research conducted over the past ten years, some points of consensus are emerging, and these will be pointed out in due course. First, however, we must look at some of the hazards accompanying this kind of research, because these affect all of us as we attempt to rediscover our history and our faith tradition as women.

17

The Vatican Council document on Revelation states: "The task of authentically interpreting the Word of God, whether written or handed on, has been trusted exclusively to the living teaching office of the Church, where authority is exercised in the name of Jesus Christ."[3] This statement refers to the task of interpretation, of pointing out and teaching authoritatively the meaning of the Word of God for today's world. On the other hand, the task of discovering what the Word of God meant to the evangelists and New Testament authors is one assigned to Scripture scholars and exegetes.[4] Today, this latter group numbers many women in its ranks. Most theological colleges include women Scripture scholars on their faculties. The task of interpreting the Word of God for the Church of today, however, is reserved exclusively to the "living teaching office of the Church." And here there are no women to be found.[5]

Nevertheless, the task of rereading the Scriptures through the eyes of women is an essential task for today's Church. And when women read the Scriptures, different meanings emerge. Women, therefore, in all walks of life must enter into the stories of the Gospels and must hear the words of Scripture with new awareness and sensitivity. This process has been compared to the experience of slavery seen through the eyes of the masters in a production such as *Gone with the Wind*, and the experience of slavery through the eyes of the slaves in *Roots*.[6] A new world and a different reality emerges when viewed through different eyes. The problems that are consequently raised for the official teaching of the Church are obvious but unavoidable.

Another obvious problem is that the Bible was written, or at least given its final form in a patriarchal culture. The cultural values of patriarchy have, then, in many places been imposed on the scriptural tradition. This is not to imply that there was a patriarchal conspiracy afoot in the early Church, but nevertheless over the years, the liberating dynamic of the New Testament was channeled into the accepted cultural forms of the day. Thus the Good News has been heard by women over the centuries as something less than positive. Sexism is the handmaiden of patriarchy, and has resulted in a fairly hostile attitude towards women and the female sex in the Churches. Much of this sexism can be traced to the Scriptures. The images of women—with the exception of Mary, the Mother of Jesus—which are most recalled from the

Scriptures are the images of women sinners. The positive apostolic roles of the women of the Gospels have not often been the subject of preaching.[7]

While sexist attitudes are apparent in the text of the New Testament itself, the way in which the gospel has been preached has further aggravated the situation. Our lack of familiarity with the women of the Gospels is sufficient proof of the way their role has not been central to our conscious spiritual life. Even as women, we have learned not to see the women of the Gospels. We have learned not to notice that women were the first witnesses of the resurrection and the first preachers of the Good News. We have learned to accept the stereotypes of the gospel women as "receptive" (Mary) or "housekeepers" (Martha) or "prostitutes" (Magdalene)—even when there is little evidence in the text for such an interpretation.

Women, then, are called on to come to the Gospels anew, as if we had never read them before. We are challenged to read with an open mind and heart. We are challenged to allow the text to speak to us directly. Like the bent woman quoted at the beginning of this chapter, we are invited to free ourselves of our bent patterns of thinking and allow the Word of God to touch us directly.

Before we begin to explore some of the new insights that are being shared with us by women scholars and believers, it may serve us well to list some of the main references to women throughout the four Gospels, without, however, making any attempt to be exhaustive.

The Gospel of Mark

Simon's mother-in-law (1:29–31)
The mother and sisters of Jesus (3:31–35, 6:3–6)
The woman with a hemorrhage (5:25–34)
The daughter of Jairus (5:21–24, 35–43)
The Syrophoenician woman (7:24–30)
The divorce question (10:1–12)
The widow's mite (12:41–44)
The woman who anointed Jesus (14:3–9)
The women on Calvary (15:40–41)

The women at the burial (15:42–47)
The women at the resurrection (16:1–8)
Mary of Magdala (16:9–11)

The Gospel of Matthew

The women ancestors of Jesus (1:1–16)
Mary, mother of Jesus (1:18–2:23)
Adultery and divorce (5:27–32)
Peter's mother-in-law (8:14–15)
The woman with the hemorrhage (9:20–22)
The official's daughter (9:18–19, 23–26)
The family of Jesus (12:46–50, 13:53–58)
Parable of the yeast (13:33)
The Canaanite woman (15:21–28)
The divorce question (19:1–9)
The mother of Zebedee's sons (20:23–23)
Parable of the ten bridesmaids (25:1–13)
The woman of Bethany (26:6–13)
The women at Calvary (17:55–56)
The women at the burial (27:57–61)
The women at the resurrection (28:1–10)

The Gospel of Luke

Elizabeth (1:5–25)
Mary (1:26–38)
Mary and Elizabeth (1:39–66)
The birth of Jesus (2:1–20)
The presentation of Jesus (2:22–32)
Anna, the prophetess (2:36–38)
The childhood of Jesus (2:39–52)
The widows of Israel (4:25–27)
Simon's mother-in-law (4:38–39)
The widow of Nain (7:11–17)
The woman who was a sinner (7:36–50)
The women disciples (8:1–3)
The family of Jesus (8:19–21)
The woman with the hemorrhage (8:43–48)
The daughter of Jairus (8:40–42, 49–56)
Martha and Mary (10:38–42)
The bent woman (13:10–17)

The woman and the coin (15:8–10)
The stubborn widow (18:1–8)
The widow's mite (21:1–4)
The mourning women (23:26–32)
The women at the burial (23:55–56)
The women at the resurrection (24:1–8)
The rejected women (24:9–11)

The Gospel of John

The wedding at Cana (2:1–11)
The woman of Samaria (4:1–42)
The woman accused of adultery (8:2–11)
Martha and Mary (11:1–54)
Mary of Bethany (12:1–8)
The mother of Jesus (19:25–27)
Mary of Magdala (20:1–18)

Although some stories are common to two or more evangelists, the impact of the stories is never identical. The repetition of the names of Mary of Magdala, Martha, and Mary, and the repetition of incidents, such as the anointing of Jesus, shows how important these stories were to the early Christians. The same can be asserted of the common testimony of all four evangelists to the women as first witnesses of the resurrection. A simple listing of references to women in the Gospels does not necessarily signify anything beyond the presence of women in the texts and, therefore, in the memories of the early Christians. It is obviously impossible here to catalogue the great amount of research that has been done on these passages. Just a few stories have been chosen to highlight the insights and challenges contained in a new reading of the texts by women. Before doing so, however, we can point to some of the general conclusions reached by women Scripture scholars in their analysis of these stories and of the whole gospel tradition.[8]

1. There is no indication that Jesus ever, either by word or deed, treated or considered women as inferior. On the contrary, by both word and deed Jesus invited women to be full members of the kingdom. The demands on women and men disciples were the same—"hearing and doing the will of God." There is no evidence that Jesus made any exception to this position.

21

2. Jesus set out to restore Israel, to bring about a "new creation." Women were included in this new creation with the same rights and privileges as men. In many instances, Jesus is portrayed breaking the Jewish Law in order to make this point clear.

3. In order to understand clearly the prophetic proclamation of Jesus, we need to recognize that he was proclaiming a discipleship of equals. This is the core proclamation. The social, familial and cultural structures of the day with their built-in relationships of domination for the males and subordination for the females soon swamped this dynamic proclamation. The sense of equality was affirmed regarding the origin and destiny of all human beings. However, in the societies in which the Church took root and in the Church, patriarchal tendencies prevailed.

4. The vision of equality did not die but remained as a creative source of tension all through the early years of the Church. In order to illustrate his message of equal discipleship, Jesus had preached the Good News to those who were excluded from the religious structures of their day. Women figured prominently in this group and the stories of women in the gospels give ample testimony to the special regard of Jesus.

5. It is clear that Jesus envisaged the new community to be "the gathering of the ungifted"[9] who, empowered by the Spirit, would bring into being the new community. To some, this might sound a subversive note, but there is no escaping the reality in the Gospels of what Elisabeth Schussler Fiorenza calls the "solidarity from below."[10] As mentioned earlier, the question of the role of women was part of the question of justice and liberation for all from the very roots of the gospel tradition.

6. This radical new vision proclaimed by Jesus was remembered by the early Church sometimes in brief pithy sayings, sometimes in lengthy parables. Many of the parables are paired, one to illustrate the point for the men in the audience, one for the women. These pairings occur frequently enough to be quite impressive in their testimony to the sensitivity of Jesus not only to the lives and concerns of women, but to their presence among his disciples. In Jesus' vision of the kingdom, the idea of women as disciples was taken for granted.

7. One set of these sexually paired parables needs special emphasis, because it is unique in the official teaching of the Church. The parable occurs—this time in a set of three—in the fifteenth chapter of Luke. The first and third are very familiar— and deservedly so—to all Christians, namely the stories of the lost sheep and the prodigal son. In the third, the story of the woman and the lost coin, Jesus compares God to the woman. The woman sweeping diligently for her lost coin stands for God. Jesus does not shun feminine imagery for God, just as he does not hesitate to use feminine imagery to describe his own love for his people.[11]

8. Discipleship is one of the keys to understanding the response Jesus asks of his followers. In Luke's Gospel, the model for such discipleship is Mary, the Mother of Jesus—a woman role model. The same is true in John. At the foot of the cross stand two persons who are to model the membership and the relationships in the new community. Already in the Gospel they bear symbolic names—the beloved disciple and the mother of Jesus.[12]

9. The Gospel of John adds other women to this picture of discipleship—the woman of Samaria, Martha and Mary, Mary of Magdala. Indeed the evangelist seems to be at pains to correct the image of discipleship already prevailing in other Christian communities. He seems to be trying to restore the role of women to its proper place in the community on an equal footing with male disciples. In the Gospel of John, three women in particular play important roles in this regard. To the Samaritan Woman Jesus reveals some of the secrets of the kingdom. She is sent as the first apostle to the gentiles to preach these mysteries to others. On the lips and from the heart of Martha comes the words of recognition of the identity of Jesus, the key act of faith which in each of the evangelists is seen as a high point in the narrative: "You are the Christ, the Son of God." The Gospel of John places these words on Martha's lips; the other evangelists attribute them to Peter. And finally to Mary Magdalene belongs the privilege of being called by name. She is named as one of "his own," a category which with other evangelists is reserved for the Twelve.[13]

10. In conclusion, it can be stated with certainty that Jesus did not accept the prevailing ways of relating to women as inferiors. There are far too many incidents in the Gospels which attest

to his respect for women and his full acceptance of them as disciples on an equal footing with men. Furthermore, this was not a casual or occasional gesture, but seems to have been a central part of the message of Jesus. The new community was preached first to those who were specifically excluded from existing communties or lived on the fringes. The friendship extended by Jesus towards women, and to Jesus by women, was not something covert or concealed. On the contrary, he constantly drew attention to it by breaking the law in order to demonstrate his regard for them. Theologians read in the Gospels today that Jesus made, and challenges his followers to make, a "preferential option for the poor."[14] No less can be said of women. Jesus made, and challenges his followers to make, a preferential option for women.

We come now to explore in greater detail five vignettes of women disciples and apostles as illustrated by the four evangelists. In the following chapter, the ministry of women in the early Church will be examined. This section concentrates in a special way on the relationship between Jesus and these women and on the roles assigned to them by Jesus as related in the gospels.

The Bent Woman

(Luke 13:10–13)

The first part of this story is related at the head of this chapter. The very first words are remarkable. Jesus was teaching in the synagogue. It was the sabbath. "And there was a woman. . . . " No explanation is given, but we are forced to ask how this woman came to be in a gathering that included only men?[15] Had Jesus summoned her into the men's section or had he moved deliberately into the women's section? At any rate Jesus saw her, included her, counted her among those present, spoke to her publicly, went to her, touched her and healed her. All on the sabbath, and all forbidden activity for a rabbi at the time of Jesus. His words, too, are startling: "Woman, you are freed. . . . " The whole scene is powerfully drawn—the bent woman in a hostile environment being freed by Jesus after eighteen years of suffering. One can imagine the hush such a scene would cause in one of our Sunday morning liturgies. Everything came to a standstill because Jesus noticed a woman in need, a woman who was bent and he freed her and she "was made straight." And as a straight woman

24

she sang the praises of God. The healed woman did not take the first opportunity to disappear as quickly as possible. No, she stood there in her new straightness and glorified God.

And what a commotion she caused! The story continues:

> But the ruler of the synagogue, indignant because Jesus had healed on the sabbath, said to the people, "There are six days on which work ought to be done; come on those days and be healed, and not on the sabbath day." Then the Lord answered him, "You hypocrites! Does not each of you on the sabbath untie his ox or his ass from the manger, and lead it away to water it? And ought not this woman, daughter of Abraham whom Satan bound for eighteen years, be loosed from this bound on the sabbath day?" As he said this, all his adversaries were put to shame; and all the people were rejoiced at all the glorious things that were done by him.

The leader of the synagogue made distinctions, divisions; Jesus went out of his way to include, to break down barriers, and in a most dramatic fashion. In the confrontation recorded here, Jesus not only asserted the rightness of the healing that has just occurred, he went further and called the woman a "daughter of Abraham." Nowhere else in the New Testament is this name used. We hear of "sons of Abraham," but this special naming of a needy woman considered by others to be in bondage of Satan, shows clearly the attitude of Jesus towards all women. Women are a part of the family of Israel. They are part of the community. They are to be counted. They are full human beings.

There was some truth on the side of the leader of the synagogue—such things had not been done before. The sabbath was sacred. The Book of Numbers recalls the incident of a man who was stoned to death for gathering sticks on the sabbath.[16] What Jesus had done, then, was extraordinary—but extraordinary only if women were considered of less value than animals. As Jesus points out, animals could be cared for on the sabbath, then why not this "daughter of Abraham?"

This incident is so extraordinary that it has led some exegetes to believe that part of the Gospel of Luke was written by a woman.[17]

A Woman Named Martha

(Luke 10:38–42, John 11:1–44)

> *Now as they went on their way, he entered a village; and a woman named Martha received him into her house. And she had a sister called Mary, who sat at the Lord's feet and listened to his teaching. But Martha was distracted with much serving; and she went to him and said, "Lord do you not care that my sister has left me to serve alone? Tell her then to help me." But the Lord answered her, "Martha, Martha, you are anxious and troubled about many things; one thing is needful. Mary has chosen the good portion, which shall not be taken away from her." (Luke 10:38–42)*

> *"Now Jesus loved Martha and her sister and Lazarus . . . When Martha heard that Jesus was coming, she went and met him, while Mary sat in the house. Martha said to Jesus, "Lord, if you had been here, my brother would not have died. And even now I know that whatever you ask of God, God will give you.". . . Jesus said to her, "I am the resurrection and the life.". . . She said to him, " . . . you are the Christ the Son of God, he who is coming into the world." (John 11:1, 20–22, 25, 27)*

This is another of those episodes thought by exegetes to have, perhaps, been preserved and written by a woman, perhaps even by Martha's sister, Mary, who plays the role of the woman theologian in Luke's Gospel. She was rather a theological student of the rabbi, Jesus, and "listened to his teaching." Whatever the origin of the story, the two accounts present us with two differing pictures of Martha. One has been remembered—Martha the busy housekeeper. The other, Martha the believing disciple, has not entered the consciousness of the Christian community. One reason for this is that the story is intertwined with the powerful account of the raising of Lazarus. Another reason perhaps is that this story, as Raymond Brown points out, is probably intended as a corrective to the exclusive attention by some Christian communities to the role of Peter. What Peter proclaims in the other Gospels, Martha proclaims here.[18]

Generations of Christian women have heard and internalized the usual interpretation of the Lucan account of Martha and

Mary. Mary the theological student became Mary the contemplative, the model nun who had "chosen the better part." Martha the housekeeper, "distracted with much serving" and complaining of her lot was rebuked by Jesus, however gently. "Martha, Martha, you are anxious and troubled about many things." And hence the advice given to generations of Christian wives and mothers to be a little less like Martha and a little more like Mary. This advice was rendered to women for centuries in a culture which said that the only place for women was in the home. No wonder the spiritual lives of women give evidence of some confusion about their roles.

Elisabeth Moltmann-Wendel has studied the role of Martha in the gospels and in later Christian tradition, and her research has produced an image of Martha which differs considerably from the Martha of popular homiletic discourse. Due to space, only a few highlights of this research can be included here.[19]

History has not been kind to Martha. Martha's complaint to Jesus in Luke's account has echoed down the centuries and has taken on a note of whining. Christian writers in the past have not spoken kindly of her. When real Christians were seen to be celibate Christians, the work of Martha was "punished and counted as nought."[20] The expression, "a Martha type," became a part of our language and denoted a person seeking a kind of resentful fulfillment in housework. A Religious community was founded whose sisters until recently were devoted especially to caring for the housekeeping needs of priests. In England today there is a Martha Movement which was founded especially to oppose the feminist movement for the liberation of women. In a word, the Christian tradition has recorded no hymns to Martha. Her holiness belongs to the lower realms.

The two Martha stories, one in Luke, the other in John, tell different stories. They are alike in their delineation of the difference in personality between the two sisters. Mary seems quiet and withdrawn; Martha is active and outgoing. This is particularly clear in John's story. Lazarus had been dead for some days. Jesus had been summoned and, as his arrival is announced, Martha rushes to greet him. This time it is she who rebukes Jesus for his delay, professes her faith in his power with God and challenges him to ask everything from God. In the ensuing conversation, Jesus reveals to Martha the mystery of the resurrection and draws from her an even deeper profession of faith: " 'Yes, Lord; I believe that you are the Christ, the Son of God, he who is coming into the world.' " Martha knows that she has said all that needs to be said and has heard all she needs to hear.

The story continues: "When she had said this, she went and called her sister Mary, saying quietly, 'The Teacher is here and is calling for you.' And when she heard it, she rose quickly and went to him." Mary and Jesus wept together for their brother and friend, and then proceeded to the tomb. No dialogue between them other than the initial greeting is recorded. Mary, in this instance is, again, the quiet one. Once again, Martha intervenes as Jesus makes for the tomb. Despite her love for her brother and her hope in Jesus, she cannot help commenting on the state of the corpse.

Martha stands out for us as the ideal model of active women in the Churches. She does not keep silent in the Church. She does not leave theology to the theologians. She wants to talk, to debate. She challenges and struggles with Jesus. For Martha, theology is learned and done in dialogue as part of the stuff of living—a surprisingly modern image, dear to the hearts of twentieth century Christian feminists. Martha is one of several stubborn women in the Gospels who encounter Jesus and engage in dialogical combat with him. They do not fit the feminine stereotypes and perhaps this is the reason they have not been remembered.

Martha's stubbornness is rewarded with one of the most profoundly important revelations in the New Testament: "I am the Resurrection and the Life; she who believes in me though she die, yet shall she live, and whoever lives and believes in me shall never die." Martha responds with her profession of faith: "You are the Christ, the Son of God." For the early Church, to confess Christ in this way, as Peter had done, was the mark of an apostle. Here, Martha, the apostle and theologian makes that profession. Raymond Brown's comment is worth quoting in full:

> Thus, if other Christian communities thought of Peter as the one who made a supreme confession of Jesus as the Son of God and the one to whom the risen Jesus first appeared, the Johannine community associated such memories with heroines like Martha and Mary Magdalene.[21]

From John's story, we can return to Luke's and perhaps see there a different Martha. It is implied that she owned the house—"a woman named Martha received him into her house." It is she who welcomes Jesus and cares for him. There is no doubt that in Luke's story Mary's role is given preference, but is this not, perhaps, because it is quieter and less disruptive? As Elisabeth Moltmann-Wendel says, John's story opens up for us the image of "aggressive, disturbing, sage, active Martha who went against all the conventions: mistress of the house, housewife, apostle, the woman who stands beside Peter in her own right."[22] There is no need however for competition between the varied images of women presented here. Luke gives pride of place to Mary, the theological student, the close friend, who follows Jesus as Teacher. This is, in itself, an enormous breakthrough for women in a culture where studying Scriptures and engaging in the intellectual life or acquiring any kind of "religious authority" was reserved for the rabbis.

John's story gives pride of place to Martha, the strong believer with the apostolic proclamation on her lips. Both were remembered in the Christian communities. Both deserve to be remembered by us. Neither gives any reason for assigning inferior roles and auxiliary ministries to women in today's Church.

The story of Martha survived in art in a rather extraordinary fashion. She is shown as a dragon slayer. George we have remembered, Martha we have not. Martha defeated the dragon, seen as the "embodiment of evil, the demonic and the old order." Martha is shown victorious over evil because it was to her that the revelation of the resurrection was made. What a change it would make to our kitchens if the harried Martha is removed and the dragon-slayer is installed in her stead![23]

The Woman Who Anointed Jesus

(Mark 14:3–9, Matthew 26:6–13, Luke 7:36–38, John 12:1–8)

And while he was at Bethany in the house of Simon the leper, as he sat at table, a woman came with an alabaster jar of ointment of pure nard, very costly, and she broke the jar and poured it over his head. But there were some who said to themselves indignantly, "Why was the ointment thus wasted? For this ointment might have been sold for more than three hundred denarii, and given to the poor." And they reproached her. But Jesus said, "Let her alone; why do you trouble her? She has

done a beautiful thing to me. . . . She has done what she could;
she has anointed my body beforehand for burying. And truly
I say to you, wherever the gospel is preached in the whole world,
what she has done will be told in memory of her."

This is Mark's account of the incident. It is the closing words of this account which Elisabeth Schussler Fiorenza took as the title of her monumental book on the Christian origins of women. It is titled *In Memory of Her.* Never again will we be able to read this story without remembering, as Jesus asked, the nameless woman of the anointing, and without remembering Elisabeth who taught us to remember. My comments on the passage depend, in large part, on this book.[24]

This scene takes place in Mark's gospel as the storm clouds of the passion threaten to break around Jesus and his little band of disciples. Three disciples figure prominently in the account—Judas the traitor, Peter the denier, and the nameless woman who anointed Jesus. Judas and Peter are remembered but not the woman. Even her name was not recorded. And in the forgetting the record has been unfaithful to what is presented as a last request of Jesus.

All four Gospels record this scene with some variations. The basic story is the same: a woman anoints Jesus; those gathered around reproach her for the deed; Jesus accepts the gesture. In Mark's account, a woman takes a costly ointment and anoints the head of Jesus. Jesus' response shows that he understands the anointing as a prophetic act. Those who reproach her are not specifically identified. The account in Matthew differs in one important instance. The reproachers are identified as disciples. Thus the contrast between them and the woman is underlined.The woman understands the meaning of discipleship; the other disciples do not. It is the woman who is identified by Jesus as the true disciple.

Luke makes some significant changes in the story. The woman becomes a sinner; she washes, dries, kisses and anoints the feet of Jesus as an act of repentance. It remains a prophetic statement about the nature of true discipleship, and calls to mind the washing of the disciples' feet by Jesus. The story however does not have the same significance as the Marcan account, and the instruction to remember the woman is omitted. John names the woman as Mary of Bethany, sister of Martha and Lazarus, and her act of anointing is the act of a loving friend.[25]

Mark's story is situated at a crucial part of the gospel. In the section before, the male leaders are plotting to arrest Jesus. In the section following, Judas sets out to betray Jesus. In between these two stories of rejection by men is the story of a nameless woman disciple who affirmed the mission of Jesus. Mark relates how the male disciples misunderstood the mystery of the suffering Messiah. Here by prophetic gesture, a woman revealed the true nature of the mission of Jesus. Her action takes the death of Jesus from the political sphere and highlights the true religious meaning. Her action is in line with the prophets of the Old Testament who anointed the head of the king.[26]

It is this action by a woman which names Jesus, an act as truly significant as that of his baptism. And the new name for Jesus is the Christ, the anointed one. "The unamed woman who names Jesus with a prophetic sign-act in Mark's Gospel is the paradigm for a true disciple. . . Both Christian feminist theology and biblical interpretation are in the process of rediscovering that the Christian gospel cannot be proclaimed if the women disciples and what they have done are not remembered."[27] This scene represents no less than another Last Supper.

Here is the story of another decisive woman, who communicated her love of Jesus, her discipleship, and her prophetic insight by deed. As has been seen, the New Testament proclaims the full equality of many of these women and, in their name, of all Christian women.

The Samaritan Woman

(John 4:1–42)

> *There came a woman of Samaria to draw water. Jesus said to her, "Give me a drink." . . . The Samaritan woman said to him, "How is it that you, a Jew, ask a drink of me, a woman of Samaria?" . . . Jesus said to her . . ."God is spirit and those who worship him must worship in spirit and truth." The woman said to him, "I know that Messiah is coming (he who is called Christ); when he comes, he will show us all things." Jesus said to her, "I who speak to you am he." . . . Many Samaritans from that city believed in him because of the woman's testimony. (John 4:7, 9, 24–26, 39)*

Raymond Brown, among others, has drawn our attention to the important roles assigned to women in the fourth Gospel.[28] The Samaritan Woman is especially significant, because, here again, Jesus violates the code of behavior regulating the interaction of men and women in Judaism. He sits by the well, asks for a drink of water and engages in conversation with her. Even the woman herself is astonished: "How is it that you, a Jew, ask a drink of me, a woman of Samaria?" The disciples returning from their shopping errand are shocked: "They marvelled that he was talking with a woman, but none said 'What do you wish?' or, 'Why are you talking with her?' " That she is a woman of Samaria only complicates the situation because these women were, in a graphic Jewish phrase, "menstruants from their cradle." Jesus demonstrates his profound indifference to all such racist and sexist attitudes by simply asking for a drink of water.

In John's Gospel, this woman is one of those key figures who lead others to Jesus because they believe "on her word." This is the same expression used in the priestly prayer of Jesus at the Last Supper when praying for his disciples: "I do not pray for these only, but also for those who believe in me through their word." Through the words of the woman, "many Samaritans from that city came to believe in him." True, as the text relates, they eventually came to faith based on the words of Jesus, but the point of the text is that the woman led them to Jesus.

The woman of Samaria has an explicit missionary dimension. She is, in fact, the first missionary to the gentiles. This is made clear by the comments of Jesus when urged by his disciples to eat: "I have food to eat of which you do not know," and further, "lift up your eyes and see how the fields are already white for the harvest." This is mission language, the kind we often hear on Mission Sundays and in prayers for priestly vocations.[29]

We may ask what the Samaritan woman was preaching. She herself had made the journey from curiosity to deep faith in the course of a lengthy encounter with Jesus. She had come to recognize him as the Messiah. Jesus said to her, "I who speak to you am he." Here again, one of the central truths of the Christian faith is revealed to a woman, and a woman who would have failed any morals test for employment in any Christian institution in the world. She had been asked for a drink of water and in return she had received "living water." This she set out to share.[30]

32

The Adulterous Woman

(John 8:2–11)

Scripture scholars are in general agreement that this story was not authored by John.[31] It does, however, fit in with the general features of the Gospels. In the *Revised Standard Version* the story is written as a footnote, and it is from this that we quote:

> Early in the morning he came again to the temple; all the people came to see him, and he sat and taught them. The scribes and the pharisees brought a woman who had been caught in adultery and placing her in the midst, they said to him, "Teacher, this woman has been caught in the act of adultery. Now in the law, Moses commanded us to stone such. What do you say about her?" This they said to test him. . . Jesus bent down and wrote with his finger on the ground. And as they continued to ask him, he stood and said to them, "Let him who is without sin among you be the first to throw a stone at her." And once more he bent down and wrote with his finger on the ground. But when they heard it, they went away, one by one, beginning with the eldest, and Jesus was left alone with the woman standing before him. Jesus looked up and said to her, "Woman, where are they? Has no one condemned you?" She said, "No one, Lord." And Jesus said, "Neither do I condemn you; go, and do not sin again."

The whole point of reading Scripture through the eyes of a woman is seen in the title given to this incident by one woman exegete: "Jesus and the Adulterous Men." She adds: "A woman reader or listener to this story may be granted an inward smile of amusement. A woman thinks: How could the woman be caught? It may not be apparent to everybody, but to a woman the act of adultery takes two."[32] One is reminded of many a contemporary discussion of prostitution. The presence and participation of men in the act of prostitution is usually forgotten.

Another reminiscence illustrates the same point. Many years ago as I was researching the position of women for my doctoral thesis, I found the following explanation of this passage. It was included in the Scriptures, the commentator gravely concluded, because otherwise we would not have known that Jesus could write. So much for the "eye of the beholder."

33

The scene is dramatic. Men interrupt the teaching of Jesus in order to test him. The gathered crowd as well as the rock-throwing scribes and pharisees await the response of Jesus. It is a particularly cruel and callous scene. The woman is a pawn, a sex object; she is entirely disposable. Her life rests in the hands of Jesus, and is of no interest to anyone beyond her use as bait for the entrapment of Jesus. As usual, Jesus changes the whole picture. He enters into relationship with the victim. He sees the woman, a human being; counts her as an actor in the event, not an object; includes her in the discussion. Her guilt is not discussed with anyone but herself. Jesus refuses to allow her to ostracize herself. She has no words until Jesus addresses her and frees her from her condemned state. In his eyes she is not godforsaken.

What of the men? Jesus refused to countenance their duplicity, their hypocrisy, their self-righteousness, their double standards, their self-established right to violence against the woman. His point was abundantly clear. The men depart without a word. No dialogue takes place. The men are not ready for a relationship with Jesus. They follow the eldest as he leads the way from the scene.

The final scene is heart-warming in its drama. "Has no one condemned you?" "No one, Lord." "Neither do I." . . . The woman is freed from her sin, from her past. She need no longer play the part of a victim, a pawn, a sex object. The words are extraordinarily moving: "Jesus looked up and said to her." . . . No threats about the stones next time. No thundering declamations about sex and women and Eve. No invitation to preachers over the ages to denounce all sexual acts as gravely sinful. Jesus looked up at her, not down on her.

Yet, there was a command: "Go and sin no more." But a command that also held in it a word of hope, a promise, a renewed strength. Reconciliation had taken place. The woman was offered the possibility of a sinless future.

And what of the men? Are they freed? Do they acknowledge their sin? They too go away without penalty, but as Jesus remarked in another parable, this one "went home again at rights with God," while the others did not.

Other stories of women are discussed elsewhere in this book—the Syrophoenician Woman, Mary of Magdala, and the women of the resurrection. Their stories are, if possible, perhaps

34

even more significant than those already related. It remains to review briefly the role of women exemplified in these five scenes:

1. The bent woman who is made straight in the midst of the worshipping community illustrates the inclusion of women in the community of coequal disciples founded by Jesus. Sons of Abraham and daughters of Abraham gather together without distinction.

2. Martha, the dragon-slayer, the woman with the apostolic mission to preach the resurrected life. She is, too, the theologian who does theology while engaged in the routine stuff of living. Her voice must be heard.

3. The woman who anointed Jesus is the revealer of the mystery of Christ. How strange to hear in the Church today that women cannot image Christ when the Gospel tells us that it was a woman who, through her act, pointed to him as the anointed one.

4. The woman of Samaria, the first missionary to the gentiles who led people to faith in Jesus on her word. What a challenge to a new generation of women apostles and women preachers!

5. The adulterous woman, raised from nonbeing to fullness of personhood by the forgiveness of Jesus. She remains a challenge to all women to refuse to participate in the stereotyping of a society which often degrades women and a Church which still debates the full membership of women.

Chapter 3

A Ruler over Many

As has been seen, in the intention of Jesus, the new community was to be a community of coequal disciples. The ministry and life of Jesus demonstrated a preferential option for women. Though it has not yet been examined in detail here, the closing days of the life of Jesus give ample testimony to the fact that women were more than equal to the task of participating in the drama of our paschal deliverance. It is now our task to explore to what extent this community of equals continued in the life of the early Church. We do not intend here to enter into profound historical and theological analysis. Much of this work has already been accomplished elsewhere, and again, my dependence is obvious.

The intention here is to build on this foundation and to present to women, in particular, a new vision of the life and time of women in the first decades of Christianity. The usual way of interpreting this era is to see it through the eyes of Paul and Peter. Much of our early documentation—the Acts of the Apostles and the Pauline and post–Pauline literature—deals almost exclusively with these two monumental figures. Other ministries and all other personalities seem peripheral or derivative.

This is especially so in the case of women because the commonly accepted theory is that their place in the Christian dispensation is secondary. When the texts are read with this foregone conclusion, that is precisely what is discovered. However, when the texts are read through a different eye, when attention is paid to what the texts actually say, a new picture emerges. We have no intention of trying to prove that women were the most important members of the growing Church. It is a fact, though, that they were the most numerous members. And it is also a fact that the ministries of women continued, at least for a few decades, with all the power and influence that they had been given in the life of Jesus.

This new vision is important for women in the Church today. It is so difficult for us to see the Church from a radically new perspective. All we have learned to hope for is a prying open of a few doors, a legitimation of a few more ministries, a permission to hope. What is needed is a quantum leap into a new dimension, a new vision of what is possible, a new understanding of Church and ministry, a new sense of having been inextricably involved with our Church's story from the beginning. We need a vision of what a Church of coequal disciples might look like. We need some guidelines toward finding our place as full members of the Church. The early years of the Church will give us this vision. It will not give us the solutions for today's Church. As Stendahl remarked, "We are not first century semites."[1] It is not a question of recreating the Church of the first century. But it is a question of seeing how we as women might take our place in a Church where we are not acknowledged as equals, even as we attempt to exercise our various ministries as fully human, fully Christian, fully baptized members of our communities. This vision is provided by the early Church.

Indeed, there were women ministers in the Church before the conversion of Paul, during the ministry of Paul, and after the death of Paul. Paul himself acknowledged this fact. This chapter is entitled with the words which he used to describe one of these mighty women who were, in Chrysostom's words, "more spirited than lions"—"I commend to you our sister Phoebe, a deacon of the Church at Cenchreae. Give her, in union with the Lord, a welcome worthy of the saints, and help her with anything she needs: for she has been a ruler over many, indeed over me."[2] The picture of a woman as Paul's superior is surely one to rejoice the hearts of all Christian women with a new vision of possibilities.

There are twenty years, crucial for the understanding of Christianity, for which we have only scant information. It is acknowledged by all that our reconstruction of this period is based in large part on conjecture. Nevertheless, we are not entirely without help. The twenty years immediately following the death and resurrection of Jesus are available to us through later reflection. Luke's history of the early Church and Paul's letters are our main sources, but both come from the period closer to A.D. 60. However, their reflections on the early years do give us some clues as to the life and lifestyles of the first generation of believers.

We are told that after the ascension several Jewish women followers of Jesus gathered with the apostles, with the relatives of Jesus, and with Mary, mother of Jesus. It is, presumably, this same group that was present at Pentecost when tongues of fire came to rest "on each of them." Then "they were all filled with the Holy Spirit, and began to speak foreign languages as the Spirit gave them the gift of speech." Women continued to join the community in great numbers, and their influence must have been great. This is obvious from a negative source. We are told that Paul persecuted, imprisoned and killed many women Christians (as well as men) as he "worked for the total destruction of the Church." Paul the pharisee seems to have been especially offended by the presence and influence of women members and ministers in the Church long before his conversion. The account in the Acts of the Apostles refers to Palestinian women Christians as well as Syrian women.[3]

Another glimmer of light appears in the first homily of the new Church. It is described in the Acts as Peter's homily made in response to the charge that they were all drunk. Peter tries to interpret the event of Pentecost to the skeptical crowd and chooses the prophet Joel's words in order to communicate this momentous experience: "I will pour out my Spirit upon all flesh, and your sons and daughters shall prophesy . . . and on my manservants and maidservants in those days I will pour out my Spirit, and they shall prophesy."[4]

It seems then that the inclusive vision of Jesus was continuing. Women and men had the same vocation in the Church. Equally they received the Spirit; equally they were called to prophecy in the Christian community. This same Spirit freed them for a new kind of life. They were to be a new creation; a new kind

39

of humanity was being created by the Spirit. Paul later described this new humanity which, for later Christians, is initiated by the rites of baptism: "For as many of you as were baptized into Christ have put on Christ. There is neither Jew nor Greek, there is neither slave nor free, there is neither male nor female; for you are all one in Christ Jesus."[5] He continued, in the following chapter of the letter to Galatian Christians, to point out that it is the Spirit received in baptism which removes us from the position of slaves and makes us children and heirs to the promise.[6] This is the Christian charter. Whatever kind of exclusive language is used later, nothing can explain away the position of women outlined here as full members of the community.

This formula in Paul is responding to sentiments common at the time in both the Greek and Jewish world where Christianity was growing. "Jews as well as Greeks proclaimed their thanks that they were humans and not beasts, free and not slaves, men and not women."[7] The Christian charter of freedom placed Christians in a radically different context.

Before the list of some of the women and the variety of ministries exercised by them is explored, it will be important here to remember the criteria for fittingness to be included within the circle of apostles. The writing of Luke noted one criterion "Those who have accompanied us during all the time that the Lord Jesus went in and out among us."[8] As has been seen, this is true of many women. Two other criteria were added in Paul: having been a witness of the resurrection, and having been "sent" by the Lord himself.[9] We have not yet examined the women of the resurrection scenes,[10] but all four Gospels testify that the women were the first witnesses of the resurrection and that they were commissioned to preach the Good News to others. Most astonishing and most difficult of all to refute is the apostleship of Mary Magdalene. In her mouth is put the classic statement of the apostles: "I have seen the Lord."[11] It comes as no surprise, then, to discover that there were some early Christian communities who endowed Mary Magdalene with more authority than Peter, because it was she who was the first to proclaim the resurrection.

All of this was not unfamiliar to the group of male writers who have been collectively called "The Fathers of the Church." Origen writes of both the Samaritan woman and Magdalene: "Christ sends this woman as an apostle to the inhabitants of the

40

city, for he sets her on fire with his words." "At the end of the Gospel a woman even tells the apostles of the Lord's resurrection, for she is the first to see him."[12] Another writes: "Christ met the women and by his words sent them out; Eve becomes an apostle, women become God's apostles."[13] Augustine leaves us with a memorable phrase: "The Holy Spirit made Mary Magdalene an apostle to the apostles."[14] And a later Father, Bernard of Clairvaux, adds: "They are sent by an angel to do the work of an evangelist. They become apostles to the apostles as they hasten in the early dawn to proclaim the Lord's salvation."[15]

It is time to look, however briefly, at the ministry of some mighty women in the early Church. There is enormous variety here—even in the orthodox sources where an attempt seems from the earliest time to have been made to minimize the importance of women. There are women disciples, apostles, prophets, preachers, deacons, presidents of communities, heads of house churches, women who pray and prophesy during public worship, and many women addressed as "sisters," "co-workers" and "toilers."[16] From this great variety, just three categories have been chosen which seem of greatest importance for our purposes here, namely to open the possibility for a new visioning of women's membership in the Church. These three categories are those of house churches, missionaries, and prophets.

House Churches

One of the first institutions heard about in the Christian mission is the house church, that is, Christian communities which gathered in private homes. In many instances, the house church was the beginning of a new Christian community in a city or town. The house church "provided space for the preaching of the Word, for worship, and for social and eucharistic table sharing."[17] The frequent mention of these house churches indicates that there were many wealthy and prominent citizens who were willing to put their homes at the service of the community. It is not only that women are mentioned in this regard, but the number of women associated with these house communities is remarkable. We will confine our attention to them. In the ancient world, the house was seen as woman's domain, so it is fitting that the activities of many house churches were in the hands of women.

41

The house church seems to have been a constitutive factor in the development of many new communities. This was the center of worship, of social life, of leadership. The house and its owner was what identified the particular community. This is clear in Paul's letters: "Please give my greetings to the brethren at Laodicea and to Nympha and the church which meets at her house." "My greetings to Prisca and Aquila. . . . My greetings also to the church that meets at their house."[18] Several other examples occur both in Paul and in the Acts of the Apostles. One of the most remarkable of the latter is the example of Lydia, one of Paul's converts. Lydia was a business woman from Thyatira and the Church of Philippi dates from her conversion. In fact, Lydia seems to have been the first European convert of Paul's, and the church which subsequently gathered at her house is, in reality, the first European Church. "And when she was baptized, with her household, she besought us saying 'If you have judged me to be faithful to the Lord, come to my house and stay.' And she prevailed upon us." Later, Paul and Silas were captured, beaten, and imprisoned. At midnight an earthquake was the occasion of their release. Paul and his companions left the prison and made straight for Lydia's house, where they encouraged the Church gathered there and then left the city.[19]

One of the most prominent founders of a house church was the woman called Prisca (or Priscilla) and her companion, Aquila. Commentators have noted that Prisca is usually named before her companion. These two co-workers of Paul seem to have functioned independently of him, using their house church as a base. Indeed they are listed as having house churches in Corinth, Ephesus, and Rome. Paul spoke of Prisca, especially, with the greatest respect. Both Prisca and Aquila had risked their lives for him, and, not only he, but the whole church must show them gratitude. Though not dependent on Paul for their ministry, either as missionaries or as local leaders, their lives seem to have been constantly intertwining. One reason may be that they shared the same trade—tent-making—a good trade, it seems, for a traveling missionary. The lives of Prisca and Aquila testify to the hardships that they were willing to endure for the gospel. The couple had been expelled from Rome when the Emperor, Claudius, expelled the "Jews" in A.D. 49 and, thence, they moved to Corinth. It was this couple who welcomed Paul to Corinth. Later, they moved to

Ephesus, and Prisca, especially, was involved in preaching and catechizing there.[20]

One of the most remarkable testimonies to women in early Christianity is the list of women greeted by Paul at the conclusion of his letter to the Romans. The first of the list is Phoebe the deacon, and to her we shall return. But, in a list of some thirty-four persons mentioned, sixteen are women, eight of whom are mentioned by name. Among these are Prisca and Aquila whom we have already met and two other missionary pairs, Philogus and Julia, and Nereus and his sister. Julia is greeted as a former prisoner with Paul. She is said to be an apostle of longer standing than Paul himself. Four other women—Mary, Tryphaena, Tryphosa, and Persis—are greeted as outstanding for their "hard labor" in the Lord's service. There is nothing quite like this list in the literature of Christianity, nor in the whole of antiquity. Needless to add, there is nothing remotely similar in the subsequent history of Christianity.[21]

The first name on the list is that of Phoebe. "I commend to you our sister Phoebe, a deacon of the Church at Cenchreae . . . she has been a ruler over many, indeed over me." There has been much argument about the meaning of the word, translated here as "ruler." Most standard translations of the letter to the Romans translate it "helper." It seems clear, however, that Phoebe, the deacon, did indeed have a position of leadership in the Church at Cenchreae. When the same word is used elsewhere it indicates someone with authority in the community. There is no reason to think, or any indication, that it means anything else here.[22]

Missionaries

Christianity was spread throughout the world of the Mediterranean by traveling missionaries. Paul's onerous journeys are known to all, as well as those of his companions. The names of the women missionaries have not been remembered with the same care. But there they were traveling the highways and byways of the ancient world from Philippi to Rome to Corinth. Again, we are well acquainted with Paul's missionary model—he founded communities, preached constantly on the nature and importance of the new community, but he himself was not identified with any one community. Preaching the gospel was his model. Another model is shown by the couple already known to us, Prisca and Aquila. The beginning of their relationship with Paul is recounted in the Acts of the Apostles: "After this Paul left Athens and went to Corinth where he met a Jew called Aquila whose family came from Pontus. He and his wife Priscilla had recently left Italy because an edict of Claudius had expelled all the Jews from Rome. Paul went to visit them and when he found they were tentmakers, of the same trade as himself, he lodged with them and they worked together." They eventually traveled with him to Ephesus, and there their ways parted.[23]

Prisca and Aquila are one of many missionary **couples.** This alone distinguishes them from Paul, but they are also distinct in their manner of conducting their mission. Since they are associated with house churches, it is obvious that they did not separate the two dimensions of the Christian mission—preaching and community building. By establishing house churches, they presided over all the aspects of the mission. One remarkable example of their missionary endeavors is their work with the Jew, Apollos. He is described as being eloquent and learned, and "accurate in all the details he taught about Jesus." But he had only received the baptism of John. Priscilla and Aquila took him into their house church and instructed him in the full meaning of Christianity.[24]

Paul's preference for Priscilla was not lost on the Christians of the ancient world. John Chrysostom wrote two homilies on her, so impressed was he by the fact that Paul always mentioned her first of the pair. He wrote as follows: "It is worth examining Paul's motive, when he greets them, for putting Priscilla before her husband. . . The wife, I think must have had greater piety than her husband. This is not simple conjecture; its confirmation is evident in the Acts. Apollos was an eloquent man, well versed in Scripture . . . this woman took him, instructed him in the way of God, and made him an accomplished leader."[25]

Many other missionaries, both women and men, are mentioned, all called fellow-workers by Paul. The work of preaching and teaching the gospel was shared among women and men. Our reading of the texts and, in fact, some later texts serve to draw attention only to the male missionaries. The evidence is there that an all-male missionary effort, an all-male Christian leadership, and all-male official teaching and preaching was not the situation in the early Church.

Prophets

In the list of ministries, prophecy is second only to apostleship, and in the list of the charisms of the Spirit, prophecy is second only to love, the greatest gift.[26] Prophecy was closely associated with preaching, with missionary work. But it was also part of the life of prayer and liturgy in the Church. We are told that prophets and teachers presided at the Eucharist, that they were recognized as leaders in the community, that they were part of the official decision-making body in some communities and that, further, they were among the group who "sent" others forth on special missionary tasks.

We know also that there were women prophets in the community, and we know the importance of some of these women in their communities. Paul mentions that they prayed and prophesied in the community, and, as *prayer* means the same whether done by women or men, that must mean that some women prayed officially and publicly in the community, as well as privately. The role of the prophet was to speak for God in the midst of the community. Prophecy is a charismatic gift, and as the Church developed, the concern to regulate the use of this gift was obvious. An oft-quoted passage from the first letter of Paul to the Corinthians goes as follows: "As in all the churches of the saints, the women should keep silence in the churches. . . For they are not permitted to speak, but should be subordinate, as even the law says. If there is anything they desire to know, let them ask their husbands at home. For it is shameful for a woman to speak in the church."[27]

In the context of all else that has been written here, these words come, on the one hand, like a bolt from the blue. On the other hand, they are so familiar that they have almost lost their punch. Scholars debate their authenticity, and it is true that they fit awkwardly into the text as it has been passed down.[28] Nevertheless, whether or not Paul actually wrote these words to the Corinthians, sooner or later their equivalent would have been found. For in the closing decades of the first century of the Christian

Church, and even more so thereafter, there was a concerted effort to exclude women from active ministry in the community. This history has been well documented, and even to nonhistorians the individual Scripture passages are familiar because of their frequent recurrence in the liturgy of the Word. We mention it here because it seems likely that it is precisely in the context of prophecy that these strictures were first elaborated.

One of the most universally accepted principles of the Christian life is that the Spirit breathes where she wills. In the first Christian communities, this principle was allowed pride of place. The way in which prophecy was integrated into the life of the community was regulated, there were criteria for true and false prophets, but all were equally considered open to the full life of the Spirit. It is only toward the end of the first century that women as a group were excluded from this ministry. Gradually, prophecy generally came under the authority of the male leaders of the community, the bishops, and died out in the Church as a specific ministry. There is ample testimony that this did not happen without a struggle. Side by side with the orthodox and canonical Christian texts is a whole series of paracanonical texts which have been preserved. Decisions about which early traditions are more or less orthodox are seen to be comparatively simple today, or at least they were until recently. A mainstream orthodox tradition was canonized which governed the way the texts were read and which texts were included as "orthodox." This "orthodox" tradition sees the threefold division of Christian ministry into bishop, priest, and deacon as normative in the Church, accepts the exclusion of women from public and official ministerial roles as the revealed will of God, and in general considers males as the only humans capable of leadership.

The paracanonical literature which has been preserved to this day tells another story. And, as we have seen, the canonical and orthodox texts, read through the probing eyes of women exegetes, historians, and theologians open up a different world. The orthodox texts we have explored briefly. We shall now take an even briefer look at the vast paracanonical literature.[29] Many gospels, acts, and letters have survived from this period which were not included in the canon of Scriptures. Almost all of the extracanonical literature came from churches and groups in which women exercised significant leadership roles. Followers of Montanus and Marcion provide some examples. In these groups women were leaders and prophets and saw themselves as directly inspired by the Holy Spirit. Since the power of the Spirit to move the hearts of all was an accepted Christian principle, these groups could not initially be attacked on doctrinal grounds. Instead their leaders—mostly women—were ridiculed. A Christian apologetic soon developed about the true Christian woman which follows the pattern already laid down by Paul, and which owed more to the secular culture of the age than to what had been, up till then, traditional Christianity.

This is the aspect of the Pauline and post-Pauline literature with which we are most familiar. Though the whole subject is notoriously difficult and has occasioned an enormous amount of comment right through the history of the Church (in recent literature it shows no signs of abating), the basic lines of development are very simple.[30] Where before women were included in Christianity as full members, as equal disciples, as co-workers in ministry, from about the second century on, women were specifically and often angrily excluded and considered to be in a position of inferiority in the Christian dispensation. Since the second century, this latter view of Christianity was the one that generally prevailed. We shall examine later[31] the theological reason for this exclusion, reasons which have not altered significantly since they were first formulated.

This section, however, concentrates on the forms of Christianity which acknowledged the full membership of women within the accepted orthodox tradition. We have looked at the women who followed Jesus, the women who ministered with authority and equality in the earliest years of the Church. We shall continue to explore the lives of women who lived as Christians in the spirit of the original proclamation of Jesus. Many of these women are venerated as saints today, though in their own lifetimes they were vituperated or excommunicated.

We will conclude this section with a backward glance at one ministry of women in the early Church which survived, at least for a few centuries, and which provides a traditional precedent, should one be needed, for future decisions about the ordination of women. This ministry is the diaconate. We have seen that

Phoebe was a deacon of the Church at Cenchreae. From the context of the letter to the Romans we know that this was an important leadership function. Male deacons are also spoken of in the Acts of the Apostles, and we know even from secular sources that both men and women deacons continued to minister in the Church from apostolic times.[32]

By the middle of the second century when the threefold division of ministry was fairly common, the diaconate was seen as an ecclesiastical office subject to the bishop. The qualities required of men and women deacons are enumerated in the first letter to Timothy.[33] Both women and men were ordained to the office of deacon, and a fourth century prayer of ordination has survived the ravages of time. We know as well that both women and men were called *deacons* until the middle of the third century when the word *deaconess* was introduced. There were specific directions for the celebration of the liturgy when both women and men deacons were present: The women deacons "sit during the liturgy to the left of the bishop," parallel with the men deacons who sit to the right.[34] This arrangement is explained elsewhere: "For the bishop sits for you in the place of God Almighty, the deacon stands in the place of Christ, and do you love him. And the deaconness shall be honored by you in the place of the Holy Spirit. . . ."[35]

The rite of ordination of women deacons which survives in a fourth century version parallels the rite for men deacons. The two essentials of ordination are present in both, namely the laying of hands and the invocation of the Holy Spirit. It is instructed that the ordination of the woman deacon take place in the "presence of the presbytery, and of the deacons and deaconesses." The prayer of ordination to be recited by the bishop read, in part, as follows: "O Eternal God, the Father of Our Lord Jesus Christ, the creator of man and woman, who didst replenish with the Spirit Miriam and Deborah and Anna and Huldah . . . do thou now look upon this thy servant who is to be ordained to the office of deaconess and grant her the Holy Spirit."[36] Though many later commentators were of the opinion that this could not have been a true ordination,[37] it was understood to be so in the fourth century Church. The age of forty was set as the age of ordination in some places, and the penalties for failing to carry out the duties of deacon were outlined. As the popularity of the office declined in the church, prominent bishops ordered that, although women were once ordained as deacons, this was no longer to be the practice of the Church.[38]

Besides their presence at worship, the women deacons performed substantially the same duties as the men. These included baptizing, teaching, maintaining order during worship, and sometimes caring of the sick. With the passage of time they were limited solely to the ministry to women, and eventually, by the seventh century in the West and the eleventh in the East, the order of women deacons was eliminated.[39]

Before this chapter is concluded, a review of some of the ministries exercised by women in the growing years of the Christian Church is important. Women presided over the founding and care of new Christian communities and seem to have been able to exercise whatever ministries were necessary to foster the growth of the community. Women were recognized as missionaries and were picked out by Paul for their diligence in the spreading of the gospel. Women were prophets in the Christian community, leading their sister and brother Christians in prayer. Women also exercised the charismatic gift of prophecy in the community and, in this capacity, were understood to be the voice of the Spirit for the Church.

Women were recognized as teachers and preachers, both roles integral to the work of missionaries. Women, such as Prisca, were noted for their outstanding abilities in this regard. Women were part of missionary teams and, as such, received praise, gratitude, and affirmation from the community. And finally, women were known as deacons and leaders in their respective communities. As such, they were in communion with Paul and the other male apostles, but were not necessarily dependent on them. In a word, there were women Christians at the foundation of the Church who never thought of themselves other than as full members of the Christian community. They worked and prayed and led their communities without ever doubting their right to do this. It seemed that this was precisely the intention of Jesus. The promise of the Canadian bishops to find ways to open full membership in the Church to Canadian Catholic women, while hailed among us today as a daring commitment, would have sounded incomprehensible to our foremothers in the faith.

Chapter 4

I Am a Christian

Historians of Christianity have always tried to narrate the story of believers in such ways as to encourage, support, and enlighten the present-day community in their living of the Christian life.[1] The next three chapters will attempt to provide perspective on some powerful Christian women who, in different periods of the life of the Church, included themselves fully and consciously as members of a believing community. Despite ever increasing patriarchal tendencies, culminating in 1410 with the decree that women could not image themselves as God-like, there remained women in the Church who continued to take Jesus and his vision of an inclusive community as the charter for their own lives. The title of our present chapter comes from such a woman—Vibia Perpetua—whose claim to be called Christian was the guiding element of her life.

Throughout most of the history of the Church, we have little idea of what the day-to-day lives of women were like. There are too few sources and far too many guesses, but we do know that not much in the way of sanctity was expected from women. Virtue was seen as an exclusively male possession. When discovered in women, it was greeted with surprise and was seen as evidence of "manly" qualities even in "weak" women. Many women describe themselves as practicing unexpected manly virtues. In many Gnostic communities, and in some Christian communities, it was the virtue and practice of virginity, in particular, which was seen

51

to endow women with manly virtue. This tendency to despise the body present in the Church from the third century on, partly explains why the history of the Church was, for the most part, written as the history of men. It was a man's Church. Women played their part only by way of exception. Their lives were understood generally to be a lifelong and not very successful struggle against the carnality of their special nature.

This is a long way from the community of disciples gathered around Jesus and the community later engaged in the proclamation of the Risen Lord in the early decades of the Church's life. There were, however, two contexts within which this sense of inclusiveness, of "neither male nor female" seem, in some sense, to have survived, and these are the contexts of martyrdom and the life of virginity. From both arenas come testimonies of Christian women who would have recognized Martha and Magdalene and Prisca and Phoebe as sisters in the faith. From these we choose for our study Perpetua, the martyr, and Marcella, the monastic founder.

Martyrdom

One of the most remarkable documents to have survived from the early Church is Perpetua's own account of the days preceding her martyrdom, and an editor's account of the actual martyrdom. As Perpetua says: "I have recorded the events which occurred up to the day before the final contest. Let anyone who wishes to record the events of the contest itself, do so." Many scholars think that it was Tertullian himself who did the subsequent recording.[2]

Perpetua lived in Carthage, the North African cradle of the Christian Church, and was a young married woman of twenty-two with an infant at the breast when her story begins. The year is around 202 and the Roman Emperor Septimius Severus had just initiated a persecution of the Christian community that was specifically designed to eliminate these troublesome members of the Empire. His design was to arrest and, if necessary, kill the catechumens and their teachers. In this way, with new membership cut off, the Christian Church would soon wither and die.[3] His plans did not expect resistance such as that offered by Perpetua

and her five companions: Felicitas, her slave; Saturus, the catechist; and three other catechumens, Revocatus, Saturinus and Se-
cundulus. Perpetua was the daughter of a wealthy Carthaginian
official. Felicity was eight months pregnant at the time of their
arrest. It appears that they had been under surveillance by the
authorities at least during the closing stages of their catechumenate, and, when they proceeded to baptism, all six were imprisoned. Despite the fact that Saturus is known to have been the
group's catechist, Perpetua comes through in the account as the
acknowledged leader.

The text we have is the prison diary of Perpetua. The recent
celebration of baptism by the group, the well-known devotion of
the Carthaginian community to the Holy Spirit, as well as the
knowledge of impending death add a certain apocalyptic sense to
the document, with many visions and prophecies. Nevertheless,
Perpetua comes through as a remarkable woman of great humanity and sensitivity. Through the personal touches in her
writing we come to know her well.

Their recent baptism gave all a strong sense of the presence
of the Holy Spirit and of being personally under the Spirit's direction. Perpetua speaks of herself as being identified knowingly
and willingly with the death of Jesus through baptism. Of the
Spirit she requested but one thing, namely perserverance in the
struggle ahead.[4] She communed with God through visions and
asked for favors directly. In all of the writings of the martyrs there
is a delight in the confusion of the normal sense of strength and
weakness, death and life, one's birth-day and one's death-day,
victory and defeat, power and powerlessness. Over all there is the
sense of protest, of knowing that the commitment to Jesus Christ
outweighs in importance all other commitments. Because of this,
when the earthly kingdom demands cooperation that might con-
tradict or give counter witness to their dedication to Jesus Christ,
the only possible response is civil disobedience, resistance, and
the kind of protest that could end only in death. When the two
cities—the City of God and the City of man—came into conflict,
Perpetua and her group had no doubt as to which citizenship
should prevail. We know that many Christians did not have this
strength and that they wavered in the final testing, but in the
writing of Perpetua there is no hesitation.

53

While Perpetua and her friends were in prison, they continued to be visited by the Christian community. It seems, too, that Perpetua's mother brought in her infant son every day so that she could suckle him. The young mother describes their first days as follows:

> I was terrified because never before had I experienced such darkness. What a terrible day! Because of crowded conditions and rough treatment by the soldiers, the heat was unbearable. My condition was aggravated by my anxiety for my baby.[5] [Some deacons from the community then paid for them to be moved to a better part of the prison for a while.] I nursed my child, who was already weak from hunger. In my anxiety for my infant I spoke to my mother about him . . . I suffered intensely because I sensed their agony on my account. These were the trials I had to endure for many days. Then I was granted the privilege of having my son remain with me in prison. Being relieved of my anxiety and concern for my infant, I immediately regained my strength. Suddenly the prison became my palace, and I loved being there rather than any other place.[6]

One of her great sufferings while awaiting martyrdom was the effort made by her father, who was not a Christian, to dissuade her. She grieved for the agony she was causing him, and for the pain she caused herself by his constant urgings to escape. Assured in a vision, that only death was in store for her, she became more adamant in her Christian faith. When the date of their trial was announced, her father visited her once more "Daughter," he said, "have pity on my grey head. Have pity on your father if I have the honor to be called father by you; if with these hands I have brought you to the prime of your life, and if I always favored you above your brothers, do not abandon me to the approach of men . . . Give up your stubborness before you destroy us all."[7] Perpetua tried to explain to him that her allegiance was to God and that all things were now in God's hands.

In the middle of a meal, the group was suddenly dragged off to the hearing. Her five companions confessed their Christianity, but just as Perpetua's turn came, her father arrived to make one last effort to dissuade her. He was arrested and beaten; Perpetua confessed her faith and all were condemned to be thrown to the beasts. During the trial, she had sent her baby home. Now she

54

sent for the child, but her father refused to allow the child to be returned to the prison.

Finally, they were transferred to the prison attached to the arena where they were to meet their fate, or, in their view, receive their reward. It was customary to chain the prisoners in this place for several days. By this time the prison officials had warmed to their remarkable prisoners and allowed members of the local Christian community to visit and pray with them. Perpetua records four visions during the course of her imprisonment, the final one a vision of herself battling the devil. In this vision, Perpetua sees herself as a man. She realized that she would be battling not animals but the devil himself. "I knew, however, that I would win."[8] Her companion, Saturus, also had a vision in which, among other things, he saw Perpetua interceding for the local bishop and presbyter so that they too could join them in paradise.

One final dramatic moment helped prepare them further for the closing combat. Felicitas was being spared the fate of her companions because the law forbade the killing of pregnant women. She mourned that she was being deprived of her victory. Led by Perpetua, the group prayed for an early delivery. Sure enough, Felicitas gave birth in prison to a girl who was received and raised by her sister. During the delivery, as Felicitas cried out in pain a guard taunted her "If you're complaining now, what will you do when you'll be thrown to the wild beasts?" "Now it is I who suffer," she replied, "but then another shall be in me to bear the pain for me, since I am now suffering for him."[9]

As the final day approached, we hear of another incident which demonstrates the humanity and courage of Perpetua. Some guards had been told that the prisoners might try to escape, using magic spells, and consequently their lot had become much harder. As the "day of victory" came closer Perpetua challenged the guard: "Why don't you at least allow us to freshen up . . . since we belong to Caesar and are about to fight on his birthday? Or isn't it to your credit that we should appear in good condition on that day?"[10] The guards relented, fulfilled their wishes and once again allowed their friends to visit. The prisoners were given a free meal before their execution, and the little group tried to make it an agape.

Finally "the day of their victory dawned." They marched joyfully into the arena, all the while exhorting the onlookers to become believers. "Perpetua followed with quick steps, the darling of God, her brightly flashing eyes quelling the gaze of the crowd." Before the final combat, Perpetua recorded one more victory. It was customary to force the condemned prisoners to wear clothing associated with the pagan gods, that of the priests of Saturn for the men, that of the priestess of Ceres for the women. Perpetua refused outright to cooperate. "We've come this far voluntarily in order to protect our rights, and we've pledged our lives not to recapitulate on any such matter as this. We made this agreement with you." They were allowed to proceed in their own clothes, and they entered the arena singing victory psalms. For the women a mad cow had been chosen "so that the women's sex would be matched with that of the animal." The six friends had exchanged the kiss of peace before they went to their respective fates. Saturus died as a result of a bite by a leopard. Perpetua was finally put to the sword. Even then, the text related, the executioner, having missed once, had his hand guided by Perpetua. "Perhaps it was that so great a woman, feared as she was by the unclean spirit, could not have been slain had she herself not willed it."[11]

Though much of the language and imagery is unfamiliar to us, the character of Perpetua shines through like a beacon. Even though a new member of the faith, her sense of herself as a Christian is awe-inspiring. Awesome too is the sense of being in direct contact with Jesus Christ and with the Spirit. Her first conversation with her father while she was still with the police and before her imprisonment perhaps best illustrates this point. Perpetua knew that through baptism she was a "new creature." Her whole being had changed and nothing in her subsequent behavior would change this realization. Her father was trying to dissuade her from her resolve. " 'Father,' I said, 'do you see here, for example, this vase or pitcher or whatever it is?' 'I see it,' he said. 'Can it be named anything else than what it really is?' I asked, and he said, 'No.' 'So I also cannot be called anything else than what I am, a Christian.' "[12]

In the Christian communities of the first four centuries, there was continued tension between the immediacy of contact with God experienced by the martyrs and the hierarchically ordered life of the community.[13] This was true for all lay people, but it was particularly so in the case of women. It was the tension we perceived in the women prophets of the early Church and, as shall be shown later, in the medieval mystics. A woman's life and spirituality was so circumscribed by her subordinate position in the life of the community that often the only avenue for spiritual growth was to transcend the hierarchical Church and experience direct contact with God. The story of Perpetua and her intercession with God for the bishop and presbyter illustrate this further. The young woman Perpetua shows us a Christian convert acting in the unshakable assurance that identity with Christ through baptism means precisely that. Her life was the carrying out of this belief.

Perpetua rejected the contrary demands made by society and her family. By choosing to live as her faith dictated, she knew herself to be living the risen life. She was already part of the new creation. Perpetua lived in "anticipatory obedience" to a new vision. For her this obedience involved martyrdom. For women in today's Church, the same challenge is offered. Many women feel that their spiritual lives are not supported and reinforced by a Church which still, for the most part, insists on a patriarchal ordering of its life and worship. The strength, assurance, and indomitability of Perpetua assures us that where our sister prevailed, so too can we.

Throughout the narrative, the freedom claimed by the little group is obvious. There is an attitude of resistance to all forms of unjust authority.[14] Even Perpetua's father is included when he tries unceasingly to dissuade her from persevering towards martyrdom. At each stage of their trial, Perpetua insists on just treatment, and her writing records the instances where she persuades the jailers to ameliorate their conditions. Though they are preparing for martyrdom and ultimate victory, the whole attitude of the group is a nonviolent one. Violence is meted out to them, but none is rendered in return. As has been shown, that does not mean that the prisoners meekly accepted their fate. It was the consciousness of final victory which gave Perpetua her stature.

Though it is difficult for those of us who live in North America to imagine ourselves in similar circumstances, the prospect of similar persecution is no stranger to the Christians of other countries. The stories of Ita Ford, Jean Donovan, Maura Clarke, and Dorothy Kazel, martyred in El Salvador makes no less compelling reading than the story of Perpetua and Felicitas. Indeed the martyrs of the Third World have even more chilling ingredients—they are usually "found dead and their killers often bear the same name of Christian."[15] These martyrs, too, lived in "anticipatory obedience" to a vision of justice based on their reading of the gospel of Jesus Christ. The atmosphere of political repression is not unlike the world at the dawn of the third century. The killing of catechists and catechized is not dissimilar in its aim from the world of Septimius Severus. Archbishop Romero, himself a martyr, formulated this when he said that the Christian Church of today has to enter into a new commitment to the poor. "It has to suffer the same fate as the poor; disappear . . . be tortured . . . captured . . . be found dead." And among these new martyrs is the same powerful sense that in weakness there is strength.[16]

The Life of Virginity

We turn now from the highly emotional, spirit-filled atmosphere of a Carthaginian prison into the bustling, cosmopolitan city of Rome in the latter half of the fourth century. The sense of urgency and crisis has disappeared and we find ourselves in the midst of a Church which no longer need fear persecution from without. On the contrary, the Church of Rome in the late fourth century struggled against the debilitating results of worldly success. The letters of Jerome provide an accurate if caustic view of the problems of a Christianity which was becoming the mandatory faith of every Roman citizen.[17]

The intense preparation for and celebration of baptism and the occasional outbursts of imperial frustration and fury had in earlier times made the choice of Christianity a life-shattering decision. It was the mission of Jerome, and later of Ambrose and Augustine, to call the Church back to something of this original fervor. The main instrument of this renewal was to be "the white martyrdom" of asceticism.

Monasticism has been called the first great fragmentation of the Christian vocation. Under the often impassioned rhetoric of the "Fathers" of the Church, a celibate elite was emerging. To this group was applied the spirituality of the "new creation," which previously had been applied to every baptized Christian. The

Church was thus fragmented in two ways. First, the monastic vocation and life was considered to be the mark of the true Christian, and marriage was relegated to a secondary place where holiness was not expected. Second, because of the peculiar historical circumstances of the late fourth and early fifth centuries, there arose in the Church a powerful clerical elite. This elite not only enjoyed the cultural support of a patriarchal structure, but now enjoyed the added power of celibacy as the avenue to sanctity, ordination as the avenue to power and authority within the Church, and civil authority as the old Roman structures collapsed under the weight of the "barbarian" invasions. Thus, in so many different ways, the fourth century represents a turning point in the life of the Church. Our main attention here is to be devoted to the sharp distinction then drawn and still remaining between the "public" role of men in the Church and the "private" roles of women.

The development of the life of monasticism in the Church can be traced from the end of the third century.[18] Both the eremitical and communal forms seem to have originated in Egypt with Anthony and Pachomius, respectively, and both forms flourished in the ensuing years. Deserts came to take on the appearance of cities as both men and women flocked there. Eventually, the cities too provided shelter to more and more organized groups of women and men in pursuit of the monastic vocation. Though traditionally monasticism is traced to Anthony and Pachomius, nevertheless, the development of monasticism for women seems to have followed a different trajectory. It is known that from the earliest days of the Church some women had opted for a life of virginity following the example of Jesus. These women lived in their homes and continued their life of asceticism in private. They became so numerous that there were several attempts during the second and third centuries to organize them into an "order" of virgins. In many ways, their story intertwines with the story of women deacons.[19] This aspect, however, is not the concern here. There is a great deal of evidence that city monasticism of both women and men owes its origins to these women pursuing their Christian call in various cities of the Empire. Some of them are known by name. Among the best known is Macrina, sister of Basil and Gregory of Nyssa, who organized her whole family, including her mother and better remembered brothers, into a monastic community. Indeed it is Macrina who is credited with having originated what was later to be called the "Rule of St. Basil."[20]

It is to Rome, however, that we turn our attention, and to two women who truly deserve the title "Mothers of the Church." They are Marcella and Paula. These women, so different in personality, testify to the liberating power of the Spirit in the lives of women. Already by the middle of the fourth century, a vigorous monastic life for women was in full swing. It seems to have been initiated by them and to have been pursued under their own direction.

The founding mother of one of these groups was the noble woman Marcella. She was a young widow living with her mother, Albina, in the family estates on the Aventine, one of the hills of Rome which was home to the great and wealthy senatorial class. We first meet Marcella in the pages of Jerome in the last two decades of the fourth century. However, her history can be traced back to the earlier part of the century when, between the years 339 and 346, Athanasius, in the second of his five exiles, was sheltered in their home in Rome.[21] Despite her youth at the time, it seems that Marcella was the happy recipient of the story of the great hermit Anthony from his later biographer, Athanasius. Athanasius, the great patriarch, defender of orthodoxy against Arianism, must have been a powerful influence on the youth of Marcella. Marcella, about fifteen years of age, with her sister Asella, her mother Albina, and a widow friend Lea seem to have lived a life of asceticism from the time of Athanasius' visit. Her family was one of the noblest in Rome, the Marcelli, and she eventually married, as would have been expected. The union lasted a brief seven months, and Marcella resisted all pressure to remarry. A nobleman, Cerialis, proposed marriage and her response gives us some indication of the character of Marcella: "If I wished to marry, I would marry a man, not an inheritance."[22]

By the time of Jerome's arrival in Rome in the year 382, there was a thriving monastic community on the Aventine under Marcella's direction. To her house flocked many women of Rome to engage in Scripture study, prayer, the practices of asceticism, and mutual encouragement. We know many of them by name—Paula, with her two daughters, Blesilla and Eustochium, Furia, Lea, Asella, and perhaps the young Fabiola.

Soon after Jerome's arrival he lectured in Scripture to the women on the Aventine. Jerome was fresh from his own turbulent attempts at the life of a hermit in the desert of Chalcis.[23] He had come to Rome in the retinue of Bishops Paulinus and Epiphanius, and was soon thereafter invited by Bishop Damaaus of Rome to be his secretary and archivist. For the years 382–384, Jerome seems to have happily pursued both vocations, dividing his time between the Pope and the women gathered at Marcella's home. In Jerome's own words, a great throng of virgins followed his teachings, and those who started as assiduous students became, after three years, close and loving friends.[24] Jerome's letters trace the success of their studies in the Hebrew, Greek, and Latin texts of the Bible. It is extraordinary to think of this group of women discussing together the varied texts of Scripture and reciting the psalms, often in Hebrew, "with flawless accents." Marcella's personal love was for the psalms, and she literally pestered Jerome to share his expertise on the most complex and technical aspects.

Letters flowed between them, though, unfortunately, only Jerome's side of the correspondence remains today. He indicated that he often tired of her persistence in discovering the meaning of the Scriptures, and he wrote on one occasion that letters are ordinarily intended to be sources of mutual comfort and exchange of ordinary events, so that those who are absent from each other may seem to be present. Marcella's letters, on the contrary, were all business.[25] She literally "tortures" him with queries. Jerome was known for his sarcasm and his letters are abundant evidence. His translations of the Scriptures were drawing down on him the rage of dozens of scholars. He vented his grief and anger in letters to Marcella, describing his critics as "two legged donkeys," and, he wrote, "there is no point in playing on the lyre for donkeys." The letter continued: "I know that when you read this you will wrinkle your forehead . . . and would, if possible, press your finger to my lips so that I will not dare say things which others would blush to hear."[26]

It seems then, that Marcella had a calming effect on the ebullient Jerome, and that often he was as much her student as she was his. In later years, Jerome often recommends his correspondents to consult Marcella.

The Scriptures were not the only subject of Jerome's teachings—he waxed eloquent on the principles and practices of asceticism. His influence here has been of enormous importance, and not altogether positive for the future development of monasticism for women. In fact, his feverish approach to the life of aseticism changed the whole development of the ascetic life for women from a freely-chosen life pursued by women as a valid option and an avenue to education and freely-chosen spiritual pursuits, to a life seen as the one hope of salvation open to women. It was Jerome particularly who interpreted the life of asceticism for women as the second redemption that women needed from their sex. Monasticism made women capable of practicing manly virtue. The thought was not new even then, but the change of direction wrought by Jerome in the monasticism for women is still having its effects today.

There is not the time here to enter into theorizing about monasticism, but it can be said that from this period on, the life of the true Christian was seen to be the monastic life, and the life of virginity for women raised them from the sinful carnality of their ordinary life and gave them hope of sanctity. In order to repress and even destroy their sexuality and all aspects of their womanly natures, they had to rigidly control their lives by ascetic practices. In Jerome's model, this included lack of sleep, food, and bathing; constant prayer, study, and reading (of one woman he says approvingly "her knees were like camel's"); avoidance of all contact with others, even married women; and removal of all aspects of feminine appearance.[27] Marcella seems to have been one of the few women who resisted the flights of Jerome's rhetoric. It can be assumed that her monastery home was led with the same serenity and good sense that appears to have been integral to her personality.

The obvious resemblance between these monastic houses and the Church houses of the first few decades of the Christian Church are striking. Within these monasteries, women pursued their lives independently. Their studies were continuous and often extremely specialized. This little group of women were alone in the whole western world in their ability to read the Scriptures in the original languages. Though the language of the "Fathers" of the

Church in regard to women is generally oppressive and often insulting, and though the ascetic life was recommended to women as a way of repressing their "feminine natures," it was experienced by women as an avenue to freedom, to education, as an escape, often, from intolerable family situations and imposed marriages, and as an opportunity to pursue independent spiritual lives. This liberating aspect continued throughout the history of religious life for women, as did the efforts of churchmen to regulate the life and bring it under the control of the hierarchy.

In Marcella and her friends we have another vision of possibility. This group of women lived, in a different way and in a different age, the original vision of the Christian message for women. Their lives were based on their love for Christ. Now to conclude this chapter we follow one of these women who for this love abandoned the city of Rome and moved to Bethlehem to live out her remaining years.

Paula had a long history of nobility in her Roman background. When she first met Jerome at Marcella's house, she was a young widow with five young children. Her grief at the death of her husband, Toxotius, had almost killed her, and it was probably Marcella's care which saw her through. Of all the women of the Aventine, Paula was the one most intensely influenced by Jerome. They were two of a kind, impetuous, committed, and always looking upward and onward for more and better ways to serve God. The friendship of Jerome and Paula was not just decisive in their own lives and in the lives of her children, but, in a sense, it opened a whole new era in the life of the Church. Again, it is another example of the pairing in spiritual friendship of a Christian man and woman which was often seen in the early Church and which was to continue with such great effect throughout history.

One of Paula's daughters, Blesilla, seems to have been a normal young woman of her times, looking forward to marriage and family life in the wealthy surroundings of noble Roman families. To Jerome, however, this sounded like the road to perdition, and when her husband died after a brief seven-month marriage, his joy knew no bounds. Here was a new student for his ascetic endeavors. Indeed, Blesilla took to asceticism under Jerome's direction with such fervor that she was singing the psalms in Hebrew in a matter of months and her whole life-style had changed.

She wore humble garments so that it was difficult to distinguish her from the servants, tears poured down her cheeks continually, her whole appearance was of neglect. And in four months she was dead.[28] The whole of Rome was outraged, and their anger was turned on Jerome and his involvement in the ascetic movement. Tongues were wagging, he wrote, and doubt was cast on every aspect of his relationship with the women.

The upshot was that a Roman synod banished Jerome from Rome.[29] As he left with maledictions on his lips, Paula was preparing to follow him. She rejoined her mentor at Antioch, and together they toured the Holy Places. Marcella received letters brimming over with joy and enthusiasms describing this odyssey.[30] They visited the desert and Paula would dearly have loved to remain there. Eventually the pair arrived in Bethlehem and proceeded to found double monasteries, funded from Paula's vast wealth. Another Christian pair had preceded them and it was their model which served as exemplar. Rufinus and Melania had been in the vicinity for several years—their monasteries were situated on the Mount of Olives.[31] Bethlehem at this time was a small village, but even then it was growing yearly as tourists and pilgrims discovered it and often settled there. A splendid church built by Helena marked the spot of the nativity of Jesus. Between 386 and 389, Paula lived in a local inn and supervised the construction of the monasteries and a hospice for travelers, the latter built specifically because it was there that "Mary and Joseph had not been able to find shelter." It was, too, another indication of the growing number of pilgrims. The monastic quarters for men were the first to be completed and there Jerome took up residence. Paula built her convent as close to the Basilica of the Nativity as possible, with the hospice beside the main road.[32]

The basilica, itself a monument to another woman's Christian faith—Helena—was to be the focus of their lives henceforth. It was here at Bethlehem that Paula lived until her death in 404, at which time her daughter Eustochium took over the direction of the establishment and she, in turn was succeeded by Paula's granddaughter, generally referred to as Paula the Younger. Here, as Rosemary Ruether points out, are seen the elements of a matrilineal succession in the governance of the monasteries; the same was true in Melania's case.[33]

A picture of the life of the monastery, no doubt idealized from one of Jerome's letters, was written as an "epitaph" for Paula after her death on January 26, 404. The monastery was divided into three sections corresponding to the differing walks of life of the women. Here they lived and worked and took their meals separately, but came together for prayer and worship. The psalms were recited at dawn, at the third, sixth, and ninth hours, at evening, and again at midnight. The remaining hours were spent in reading and study, the maintenance of the convents, and in sewing. Each group had a leader chosen by Paula, and it was she who led the group to worship at the basilica on Sunday. All were dressed alike and none owned anything except their clothing. Paula was the overall leader and, from Jerome's description, managed her convents with skill and tact.[34]

Though the atmosphere here seems calmer than the feverish excitement of Jerome's two years in Rome, nonetheless, ascetic practices of fasting, avoiding bathing, and limited sleep still were part of their lives. Keeping in mind Jerome's tendency towards exaggeration, we can see something of their lives in the following picture from his pen: Paula and Eustochium were "shabbily and somberly clad, positive heroines in comparison with their former selves, they trim lamps, light fires, sweep floors, clean vegetables, put cabbage heads into the boiling pot, lay tables, hand around cups, serve food and run to and fro to wait on others."[35] One other thing had been learned from their Roman experience—complete separation between the women and the men was maintained, though this did not seem to include the relationship of Paula and Jerome. Jerome remarks that separation of the sexes was necessary so that "evil tongues will not slander the saints in order to reassure the sinners."[36]

It is written also that Paula and Jerome read the whole Bible through together, and, when they could not meet, their correspondence kept them in touch. Paula's last years were plagued with illness, but according to her wishes, she died in absolute poverty. Her huge wealth, after providing for her children's future, was expended in the founding of the monasteries and in extensive alms-giving.[37]

Another ancient writer, Palladius, the historian of monasticism, has left us a description of Paula. His comments are interesting: "It is necessary also to mention in my book certain women with many qualities, to whom God apportioned labors equal to those of men, lest any should pretend that women were too feeble to practice virtue perfectly. Now I have seen many such and met many distinguished virgins and widows. Among them was a Roman lady, Paula, mother of Toxotius, a woman of great distinction in the spiritual life. She was hindered by a certain Jerome from Dalmatia. For though she was able to surpass all, having great abilities, he hindered her by his jealousy, having induced her to serve his plan."[38]

Palladius may well be referring to the event of Blesilla's death and Jerome's extraordinary letter to her mother at that time. To one as ardent and ascetic as Paula, his words could indeed have provided the impulse for the abandonment of the rest of her family. Paula was devastated by the death of her daughter, Blesilla. Her health was never very good, and her companions feared then for her life. Jerome, instead of sympathy, wrote her a stinging rebuke. You must choose, he tells her: either you are going to be a saint or a sinner. The words *Christian* and *ascetic* completely obliterate the name of *mother*. If she is to continue mourning she can count herself the disciple of the devil, but not of Jerome. Her tears of grief are detestable, sacriligious, and an eloquent testimony to her lack of faith.[39] What a letter to a grieving mother from one of the leading Christians of the day! At any rate, Paula's monastic vocation continued, and eventually led her to abandon her family and follow Jerome literally, as has been seen.

In his epitaph on Paula, Jerome gave a description of her leave-taking with her family: "She reached the harbor, accompanied by her brother, relatives, friends, and, of course, her children. Already the sails were swelling, and the ship, guided by oars, was on the point of heading out to sea. On the shore stood little Toxotius, imploring with childish gestures; and Rufina, soon to be married, begged her with silent tears to linger until the wedding had taken place. However, dry-eyed, her resolve mirrored in her gaze, Paula conquered her love for her children by her love for God. She ceased to act as a mother in order to prove herself the servant of Christ. It was clear that she was struggling intensely with her sorrow, all the more admirably in that she had a great love for her family."[40]

Perhaps it is this passage, more than any other, which shows the confusion in the mind of the ascetic and illustrates the fragmentation of the Christian vision. When seen as a chosen life style, asceticism has been of enormous importance in the life of the Church. When seen as the only definition of Christianity, and when all other human and Christian duties are compared negatively with asceticism, such comparison serves only to cast discredit on the whole ascetic system. Besides, both in the passage quoted from Palladius and so often in the writing of Jerome, the complete contempt for women can be seen. Their service to the Church is praised only when they show contempt for everything that is womanly. The theology of the double redemption needed by women further emphasized their inferiority.

It is only with astonishment that we can return to a woman like Marcella who in this atmosphere continued to live her monastic life with serene dignity. The monastic vocation undertaken by her had not been in the later spirit of Jerome's horror of all things sexual and human. It was, for Marcella, a question of freedom—not freedom from womanhood, but freedom from the social restrictions placed by her environment on the life and fulfillment of women. It was this latter kind of monasticism which continued to provide the dynamism and creativity of generations of women religious, despite the fact that the Church's regulation of women religious followed more along the lines set out by Jerome.

Jerome's own life, of course, is ample testimony to this same confusion of goals and desires. His words about women are among the harshest ever written. His life, on the other hand, shows that he could not have survived without his women friends. His very contributions to the later history of the corpus of Scripture was supported, urged forward, and often challenged by his women friends, Marcella in particular. When reading the letters of Jerome, one needs to be ever aware of his penchant for branching off into mere rhetoric. His letter, however, on hearing of the death of Marcella and the circumstances surrounding her death are obviously sincere.[41]

After Jerome's departure, Marcella's monastic foundation continued to flourish. Her life followed an even tenor of prayer and study. At Jerome's suggestion, many priests and other learned men consulted her on the meaning of certain passages of Scripture. It is likely that she alone in Rome continued to be able to read the Scriptures and explain them in their original Hebrew texts. Letters continued to flow back and forth between Bethlehem and Rome, and the friendship of Jerome and Marcella continued.[42]

On one occasion Marcella emerged from her seclusion to the defense of her friend. It was a most confusing situation, dealing with the writings of Origen, and the translations of Rufinus and Jerome. The two latter men had taken different stances on the orthodoxy of Origen, and their subsequent writings continued to abuse each other. Rufinus was in Rome in 397 and as far as the friends of Jerome were concerned he was denigrating Jerome's name by linking it with heretical tendencies in Origen's work. Marcella was the organizer of the campaign in defense of Jerome; she assembled a dossier to prove his innocence and challenged Pope Siricius in person to repair the damage and condemn Origenism. The whole of Italy was dragged into the combat by the preaching of another of Jerome's friends, Eusebius of Cermona. Siricius died before the situation was clarified, and his successor, Anastasius, was personally briefed by Marcella on the nature of the controversy. She produced witnesses and new documents and succeeded in convincing the Pope to accede to her wishes. Finally in 400, Origenism was condemned, and Jerome's name was cleared.[43] Both Jerome and Rufinus had in fact contributed not a little to the whole controversy by their highly personal interpretation of the works of Origen, and both men were accused—probably rightly—of interpolating the texts for their own convenience. Unfortunately the name of Origen suffered great harm in the controversy, and this had a most unfortunate effect in later ages on the influence of the greatest theologian between Paul and Augustine.

Marcella's involvement in the controversy does not do her any particular credit, although in the heat of the battle it must have been extraordinarily difficult to discern on which side the truth lay. What is remarkable, however, is the influence she wielded with a succession of Popes. After her involvement in this fray, Marcella again retired to her convent, while Jerome seems to have continued his anti-Origenistic battles in the East. Suddenly, the world was shocked by the fall of Rome to Alaric the

Goth. The city which was the head of the world had fallen. The drama of the event is admirably conveyed in Jerome's writing; for him the world was coming to an end. The fall of Rome in 410 could mean only one thing, the sins of the wicked were being punished.

It was an added sorrow to hear of the death of Marcella. The city of Rome had been under siege for over a year and when, finally, Alaric entered the city he allowed his soldiers to plunder at will for three days. Marcella's home and its occupants fell victim to their violence. We are told that soldiers broke in searching for gold, and when Marcella drew attention to her unpretentious surroundings, she was beaten by the soldiers. Her one care was for her younger companion, Principia, and it seems that she succeeded in protecting her from the soldiers. They were eventually rescued and brought for shelter to the Basilica of St. Paul. Excavations have shown that the Aventine was badly burned and plundered at this time, so it is likely that she did not return to her home. Some months later she died with the faithful Principia at her side.[44]

Marcella's lifespan bridged the closing of one era and the opening of another. Rome, the center of the universe, changed hands, the rule of the Goths being only a temporary transition until Rome came to be seen as the capital of a new and Christian Empire. In the Rome of Marcella's day both the best and the worst of the Church were in evidence. In her own life, however, it is easy to see how the essentials of gospel living prevailed. She was a Scripture scholar, friend and adviser of saints, counselor and challenger of popes, disciple of the great Athanasius, and the first woman to found and preside over a monastery in the western Church.

Chapter 5

The Light Comes

A noted historian of the Middle Ages writes that by the closing years of the period one social axiom had become firmly established and was long to remain in force as law: "Woman's voice is not to be heard in public."[1] This law was a man's law; man was the sole authority in the family, in society at large, and in the state. That this was generally the case can be verified from any number of sources. Nevertheless, this chapter deals with two extraordinary women whose voices and lives were seen to be not only authoritative, but directed in their awesome task of leadership by God alone. They are Catherine of Siena and Joan of Arc. The fact that the two women failed signally in their allotted tasks only serves to add luster to the perseverance and God-given assurance with which they faced life in one of the most complex periods of Christian history.

They lived in different centuries, but the sense of mission, of personal call, of what today we might call *self-worth* are identical. Catherine lived from 1347–1380, and, as a young girl of twenty-two, set out to reform the Church. Joan lived from 1412 to 1431, a brief nineteen years. At the age of seventeen she set out, directed by God, to restore France to its rightful king. The tenacity of the two women is extraordinary in an age when they not only had to face questions about their personal veracity, but also accusations of heresy, diabolical influence, and witchcraft. The lives of both women seem to move in and out of this world and another world with astonishing ease. For this reason, the lives of both women have been raised to the level of myth. This is particularly so with Joan. Hers is one of a handful of names known to every school child the world over, and her legend has also left us with an immediate vision of her in soldier's dress with her eyes piercing the future.

We turn first here to Catherine, but before doing so, it will be necessary to spend some time establishing the medieval context within which these two women and their contemporaries lived.

The Middle Ages present many paradoxes, not the least in the lives of women. In an age when sex was most repressed, a creation-based spirituality and the lives of a group of marvelous women mystics grace the pages of history. Historians speak of mighty women leaders in the arenas of Church and politics at the highpoint of the period, but the lives of the ordinary women are as hidden from view as at any other period in history.[2] Because the few women brought to our attention by historians were either queens or abbesses or both, it is important to remember that for most women the disposition of their person was entirely in the hands of men. At no time in history had women the right to make personal decisions about their lives. Both marriage and virginity were the choice of husband or father. This was supported not only in Church law but also, since the time of Constantine, in civil law.[3] We have seen that organized religious life for women, though more and more rigidly controlled by the Church, nevertheless presented women with an opportunity for self-directed lives and for education. Education for women was not encouraged in principle, however, even in the convents. Learning was a class prerogative; convents of noblewomen brought this right into the convent with them.[4]

Officially, the stance of the Church and society was the one reported at the beginning of this chapter. Women were at their best when they were neither seen nor heard. It is true that the cultural changes accompanying chivalry and courtly love made it somewhat easier for women to venture abroad. Men had discovered another way of relating to women other than by rape or violence. Nevertheless, this was often more of a literary conceit than a real change for women. The **choice** of a life of virginity which was the goal of all Jerome's urgings was replaced in the middle ages by the imposition of cloister on many women who often had no vocation to that kind of life, but who were felt by society to be superfluous. The saying about silence was reinforced by the saying *aut maritus aut murus*—either marriage or cloister.[5] This setting adds new insight to the lives of Catherine and Joan, who were both lay women who resisted the efforts of others to marry or cloister them.

The tales of chivalrous knights learned in childhood bear some relationship to reality in the period under discussion, but the greatest result of the movement of chivalry was, in the words of one writer, "the house-broken male."[6] Romantic love was born and with it a new vision of social interaction. Rules of etiquette (little ethics) were elaborated to govern these new interactions between women and men, and the new emphasis on the "worship" of women from afar brought into being the role of women as love-object or sex-object. Though Christianized in subsequent history, to some extent, the whole movement was distinctly anti-Christian, encouraging as it usually did, the love of a husband for a woman not his wife. This was not new, but the idealization of the "mistress" in poetry and song was the symbol of a new era of human relationships.

The boost given to trade by the crusades and other wanderings brought in its wake a certain settling down of society. Hitherto society had been divided into classes—nobility, based on land or conquest; the clergy, based on ordination; the vast majority who were peasants or serfs. Now a fourth class was added—the merchant class. The distinction remained clear on a sign outside a convent near my home in Ireland—"For Daughters of the Merchant class," to distinguish it from a neighboring convent whose sign read "For Daughters of the Upper Class." Women of this new middle class had a new sense of security in the newly built towns. Life was less violent. Trades and crafts were practiced with more security. The towns gradually became law-abiding places.[7]

Throughout the whole Middle Ages, however, there was one obvious lack and this was the lack of care for the religious life of women, and the total suspicion with which any effort by women to supply this need was greeted. The history of the rise and suppression of the "Beguines," the "praying women," is ample testimony to this.[8] The same is evidenced in the lives of the two women studied here, for women were not deemed to have spiritual life except through the mediation of men. In the Church of that age, no provision was made for this. The imposition of cloister on religious women was one means of removing holy women from general circulation.[9] It was from these groups of Beguines that the admirable mystical tradition for women originated.

The accusation of heresy was never far away from a holy woman whether inside the convent or out. In a sense, this was a logical conclusion to the official teaching of the day about women. Women were inferior creatures. Church life was structured to exclude them. The teaching of Thomas Aquinas, based on the natural law, reinforced this teaching. This shall be explored at greater length in another part of this book, but one point can be added here. Thomas pointed out that all animals are created as equal pairs. Humans are different in that they come from one single principle, the male principle. The girl child, then is a defective human being, the result of an accident. Women, therefore, are always and everywhere auxiliary, and this subordination is part of the original design of God. For Thomas, the inferiority of women resided in their inferior bodies. Both sexes are marked by the image of God, but for the women this is so only when she is in subjection to the more "rational" male who is the image of God par excellence. Following this line of thinking, Thomas could see prostitution as a necessary and "lawful immorality." Prostitution was, he said, like "the sewer in the palace." If it were not there, the whole palace would be polluted.[10]

Many popular assumptions, both in Church and state, about women come from this period. In spite of the obvious facts of life, for example, most Church sermons preached about adulterous wives, and rarely mention adulterous husbands. The image of the good wife in popular literature was the woman who gave equal care to her husband's bastard children. The popular literature gives some insight into the home life of the women of the lower classes. The wife's domain was the house. Her virtue was shown in never asking her husband for an explanation of his whereabouts. The good wife spoke rarely and never at meals. She gave her husband complete liberty and was never jealous. Obedience was especially necessary in public. The life of women in the Church offered at least one ingredient which might redeem this bleak picture—a life of submission could be redeemed by the woman's love for

God.[11] In this context, the achievement of Catherine seems all the more remarkable. Here we shall look briefly at the story of her life, and then allow her writings to give us a further insight to her personality.

Catherine

Catherine's life was lived out during some of the most formative events of European history. In 1305, Clement V, a friend of the French king whose conniving had led to his election as Pope, took up residence at Avignon. There the papacy remained for the next seventy years—years full of intrigue, charges and countercharges, which ravaged the face of Europe, and in particular, French-Italian relations.[12] In January, 1348, while Catherine was still an infant, the black plague, which was to decimate Europe, began. Some cities, towns, and villages were almost completely destroyed.[13] In between, the disastrous Hundred Years' War between France and England had introduced paid soldiers to both countries whose violent life-style left both languages with a new world—brigandry.[14] It was a Europe and a Christendom—for they were still synonymous—which was on its knees, worn out by cruelty and famine.

Catherine Benincasa was born the youngest of twenty-five children to Jacopo Benincasa, a well-to-do citizen of Siena whose trade was dyeing, and Monna Lapa, his wife, who much later became one of her daughter's disciples.[15] Catherine was a happy child, remarkable for her joyous disposition and her beautiful golden brown hair. By the age of six or seven she was the recipient of frequent visions, and her life began to follow the pattern which initially for her family caused so much confusion and sorrow. She took a vow of virginity but resisted all attempts either to make her join a convent or marry. Her one thirst was for solitude and there seemed so little of that in the noisy home and surroundings of her childhood. Her family seems to have been so irritated at her unwillingness to cooperate in the plans for her future, that for several years they treated her as a servant in the household. Her father, Jacopo, one day found her at prayer and was so amazed at what he saw that he forbade any further interference with her vocation. Catherine became a member of the Third Order of St. Dominic and lived in her own home devoted to prayer, extraordinary penance, and solitude. This period of mystical seclusion lasted for about three years, seemingly entirely under Catherine's own guidance, except perhaps that given by a foster brother who had become a Dominican. This period closed with Catherine's experience of a mystical marriage with Christ which was to mark her entry into public life.

The next few years were spent in ministry in the city of Siena, again seemingly initiated and conducted under Catherine's own guidance. Several companions, both male and female, joined her, and the prisons, hospitals, and poor of the city all benefited from their ministrations. Her almsgiving caused havoc in her family, and finally the family possessions had to be placed under lock and key. During this time her reputation spread far and wide and, in a sense, she became the spiritual director not only of all Siena but of all Europe.[16] Some reports mention as many as 1500 of her collected letters, but only 400 have survived. There are tales of couriers lining up outside her door awaiting a response. Her correspondents included kings and princes, bishops and priests, queens and abbesses, and eventually the Pope himself.

During these years a kind of mystical school met at Catherine's house and developed their spiritual lives under her guidance. These were companions and friends who were eventually to follow her on her journeys. They included Lisa, Alessa, and Cecca, women of Siena; four priests; a poet; a recent convert; and an English monk, William of Flete, who had been living as a solitary near Siena. Some joined to atone for a former life, others sought to be close to a woman who could see "the hidden things of God."[17]

In the mid 1370s Catherine's life took a dramatic turn. She became intensely involved in three highly political, and intensely religious activities—the preaching of a crusade, the effort to force the Pope to return to Rome, and the peace-making activities between the Florentines and the papacy. Her letters and the writings of her biographer, Raymond of Capua, who had been appointed as her confessor in 1374, testify to the complexity and exhaustive nature of all these activities.[18] But from this time forward Catherine's life was committed to the reform of the Church. At twenty-three, she had found her lifework, a task which was to involve her with all the crowned heads of Europe and most ecclesiastical dignitaries of the age, including a succession of Popes.

In this period Catherine's story assumed a larger than life dimension, as she strode across the pages of history in obedience to her visions.

The details of these complex historical events need not detain us here: a brief outline will suffice.[19] Pope Gregory XI had become Pope in 1370. It was almost entirely through Catherine's influence that he finally returned to Rome in 1377. Catherine had traveled to Avignon to confront him personally—respectfully, of course—sometimes in person, sometimes through letters. Her language was direct, quite out of the ordinary for a young woman to use in address to the Pope. Catherine's whole effort was to persuade the Pope to fulfill his spiritual duties and all else would fall into place. In her second letter to him she wrote, "I have heard that you have created cardinals. I believe that it would be more to the honor of God and better for yourself if you would always take care to choose virtuous men. When the contrary is done it is a great insult to God and a disaster for the Holy Church."[20] And again she wrote: "I beseech you do what you have to do manfully." She calls him "sweet Christ on earth" and in several places "my sweet Babbo" and "holiest and sweetest and dearest Father."[21] In the midst of these sweet phrases she as much as orders him to rid the Church of unworthy priests and bishops: "The world is stinking with the immorality of the clergy."[22]

The intensity of Catherine's commitment to her task leaps off the pages of her letters: "Peace, peace, my sweet Babbo, and no more war." "Come before September if you can do so; in any case do not delay beyond September. And do not heed any opposition you may meet; but come like a virile man who does not fear. Take heed as you value your life not to come with armed men, but with the Cross in your hand like a meek lamb. Come, come."[23] "Up like a man, Father, I tell you there is no need to fear. You are bound to come: then come."[24] There are pages of this kind of writing in her final letters before Gregory made up his mind to return to Rome. One can be pardoned a smile of disbelief at her closing in one of them: "Pardon my presumption. I humbly ask your blessing."[25] Finally on September 14, 1376, the Pope left Avignon and arrived in Rome in January of 1378. A few months later Gregory was dead and the whole Church was thrown into the enormous confusion and tragedy caused by the Great Western Schism. Roman cardinals elected one Pope, French cardinals another, both apparently validly elected. If the facts still occasion debate among scholars, the confusion of the Church of the day is all the more understandable.[26] Catherine, as might be expected, supported the Roman line, and was invited by Urban VI, the successor of Gregory to address himself and his assembled cardinals. In his introduction, he said: "This weak woman puts us all to shame. I do not make little of her. . . By nature she should be the coward . . . but it is we who are the cowards and she stands undaunted."[27]

Catherine was heart-broken. All her efforts were unavailing. The schism continued. Catherine believed that the underlying cause of the schism was sin, chaos, lack of peace, lack of commitment to God's will. She offered to take the sin of the Church upon herself, suffered a stroke, and died surrounded by her little band on April 30, 1380. Catherine's life had dominated the cities of Siena, Avignon, Genoa, and Rome. At twenty-nine she had taken upon herself the reform of the Church. We conclude her brief portrait with an all too brief look at the personality of a woman who for a few years was the voice of God for Europe.

One of the words constantly on the lips of Catherine was *obedience*. It was an obedience based on love and rendered primarily to God alone. Despite her frequent professions of humility and deference when dealing with officials in the Church, Catherine was convinced that obedience was a testament to the will of God. And often her superiors were, in her view, manifestly not carrying out the will of God. She looked for peace, for harmony, for reconciliation. Her cry "No more war!" precedes that of Paul VI by six hundred years. She was determined to make the Pope worthy of her obedience. Then, in all simplicity she would obey. Pope or bishop or priest, she insisted that before they could claim her obedience, they themselves should be manifesting in their lives that obedience to God which guided her own life.

Catherine's message to the Church seems to have been conveyed, not only by her words, but by her remarkable presence. Story after story tells of people who scoffed and ridiculed this mere woman at a distance, but in her presence were overcome with sorrow at the emptiness of their lives.[28] This powerful presence flowed from her conviction of her dignity as a child of God. As such she was subject to no one but God. She moved freely in an atmosphere of what often today is called "creation spirituality."[29] With the ancient poet she could say *nihil humanum alienum—*

nothing created or temporal or human was necessarily evil. God's goodness and love were evident in every detail of His creation. It followed then, for Catherine, that self-knowledge and appreciation of oneself was fundamental to holiness. She spoke frequently of this. We owe it to ourselves to know ourselves; it is only then that we can really help others.

Catherine was in love with the truth. This was an intrinsic aspect of her obedience. She never accepted the untruthful condition in which the Church found itself. Indeed, she blamed the leaders of the Church and their vacillation for the institutional untruth evident in the exile of the Church at Avignon. She was very much aware, too, of what today is called *institutional injustice,* and challenged it both in Church and state. Catherine had a real love for the poor and often spoke of justice in their regard. Her compassion for all who were suffering in any way was legendary and is probably best remembered in the story of the condemned man whose head she held for comfort while it was being chopped off by the executioner.[30]

Catherine's life of mission had begun with prayer. Three years had been devoted exclusively to communion with God in the solitude of her home. Prayer was always central to her life, and, as was seen, during her lifetime she had become the spiritual director of half of Europe. Her advice, however, was always eminently sensible. To a priest who protested that he had little time for prayer, she wrote: "pray the prayer of action," and reminded him that the life of a good person is in itself a prayer.[31]

This is a fitting description of Catherine herself, and we close this part of her story with the words spoken to her by the Pope whose life was most influenced by her, Gregory. "In order that you may know clearly that I want peace, I leave it entirely in your hands; only remember that the honor of the Church is in your keeping."[32] It could not have been in better hands.

In 1966, Pope Paul VI initiated a process to discover whether or not Catherine and Teresa of Avila could be named Doctors of the Church. He invited a number of theologians to study the question: "Could this title be given to a saintly woman?"[33] The answers were, apparently, all in the affirmative though the theologians had studied the question independently of each other.

By 1968 the Pope had further support from the Sacred Congregations concerned and, on October 4, 1970, Catherine of Siena, laywoman, was declared Doctor of the Church.

The journey towards this day had begun many years earlier. In 1922, the king of Spain had petitioned for such an honor. The Bishops of Spain had prepared dossiers on Catherine and Teresa and presented them to the Pope. The University of Salamanca had made Teresa an honorary doctor and presented a degree to her statue. The dossiers, however, were returned, stamped by Pope Pius XI's own hand *obstat sexus*.[34] An accompanying document explained the teaching of St. Paul that a woman could not teach in the Church. It was this decision which was reversed by Pope Paul VI, and Teresa and Catherine were proclaimed Doctors of the Universal Church within a week of each other: Teresa as a representative of all nuns, Catherine of all laywomen.

What does this mean? It means that a laywoman now has the right to teach in the Church, that a laywoman has officially joined the *magisterium*, that the ancient tradition of the Church begins to sound more whole because within the chorus of voices is now, for the first time, heard the voices of women. Another vision! Another possibility!

Joan of Arc

Catherine, it is said, was taught to read in a vision by the great Thomas Aquinas himself. Only later in life did she learn to write. It is doubtful if Joan of Arc ever learned either to read or write. Joan's life, however, is the stuff of which legends are made. She came to symbolize the whole country of France, and has continued to inspire volumes of writing, mostly imaginative—drama and poetry. It is difficult to write about Joan in prose, partly because her life was so extraordinary, but also because, even to her contemporaries, she seemed to be larger than life.

Joan was a peasant, and as such differs from all other women in our study. In the Church's roster, there are a very few peasant saints. In the Middle Ages, the Church, in fact, tended to be hostile to peasants.[35] Priests and monks were ordinarily concentrated in the towns. Country priests were often spoken of as being as ignorant as the peasants themselves, the latter being described as well as violent, avaricious, and bestial. This does not mean that this is the truth about peasant life. Joan's family was pious, but the resources of religious life were not made available to them. From Joan's own life, what is apparent is that she knew the Lord's prayer and the Hail Mary and was familiar with the legends of some saints. The angels Michael and Gabriel were also known to her. At no time did Joan show any familiarity whatever with the Scriptures; she never quoted them. Her quotations of religious truths were in the form of proverbs, "God helps those who help themselves" or "A good man is often hanged for telling the truth."[36]

Neither did Joan's life show any familiarity with priests or Church life. The spiritual life of this peasant girl was built on few resources. An account of her in childhood described village festivals, a reliance on relics, and dependence on the local priest to be there only in times of natural calamity. The task of the Church, no less than society in general, was to keep peasants in their place. The advantages of culture, and of the Church, were available only to the upper reaches of society. These included the path to sanctity. Holiness was not expected of peasants, and any indication of unusual fervor was greeted with suspicion. Joan, then, began life with a double limitation—she was a woman and she was a peasant.

The society into which Joan was born was a total society— this indeed had been the Church's dream since Charlemagne. All persons and every aspect of society was under the care of the Church. The dream was that Europe would resemble one large monastery. The reality was far different, but nevertheless, the dream was perpetuated by ruthlessly keeping to a hierarchical and class-structured society. For a total society is a compulsory society. In such a society, any disruption is seen as dangerous, and, on the other hand, as each disruption is healed, the strands of life continue as before. It is no surprise then to see that the very bishops, lawyers, and judges who condemned Joan and participated in her execution, were also present thirty years later at her rehabilitation hearing. The total society continued.[37]

In Joan's time, as in Catherine's, the total society was being disrupted in a particularly vicious way by the Hundred Year's War. This conflict succeeded in creating two communities of hatred, one labeled French, the other English. It was Joan's contribution to awaken and resurrect French nationalism, and this aspect of her life has never been forgotten. It was within this conflict that

Joan played her part for two brief years, starting at the remarkably tender age of seventeen. Two years later, at the age of nineteen, her ashes had been scattered in the Seine. Our look at Joan's life will be episodic. Despite her fame, and the vast quantities of literature devoted to her, and in this case, devotion is a fitting word, few historical studies have been done. Much still remains shrouded in mystery. This account depends substantially on Marina Warner's recent eloquent work on the "image of female heroism."[38]

One of the continuing mysteries surrounding the life of Joan is how it all started. It seems that suddenly in late February of 1429, Joan arrived at Chinon to accost Charles and announce to him that she was going to restore him to his rightful heritage, the kingdom of France. In what little we know of her earlier years, nothing prepares us for this "arrival."

Joan was born in 1412 at Domremy in Lorraine. By all accounts, it was a normal village life, even ideal in some sense. At her trial later, her accusers, with their morbid fascination and overactive imaginations tried to make much of the village dances and festivals as early evidence of witchcraft. What was simple village enjoyment, became, in their hands, the work of the devil. Joan sometimes herded village animals as a child, and played in the fields with her friends. It was out here in the open that she first heard her "voices," probably in 1425 when she was about thirteen years of age. These voices became the spiritual guides of her life. There is still much that is mysterious about them. What is known of them comes from the record of her later trials and the inquisitor's persistent and fascinated curiosity about the origin of these messengers. Not unexpectedly under such relentless questioning—sometimes by as many as fifty judges at one time—her story changed. It is unclear whether Joan was holding back information, or was, in fact, being faithful to her voices in not revealing everything to her cruelly persistent judges. We are told that her first experience of the voice came from a shining cloud with the message: "Joan, you must lead another life and perform wondrous deeds; for you are she whom the King of heaven has chosen to bring reparation to the kingdom of France and help and protection to King Charles."[39]

Her examiners were obsessed with these voices—badgering her constantly about their human appearance, whether or not she touched them, whether or not she had any sensual experience of them. The judges were trying to maneuver her into admitting that her experience had something concrete to it; then to their satisfaction they could prove the presence of sorcery. Initially Joan's only response was that "The light comes in the name of the voice."[40] Eventually, she identified her voices as Saints Margaret and Catherine, two women saints whose cults were extremely popular in the fifteenth century. Saint Catherine was the patron saint of the neighboring village, and the stories of her extraordinary martyrdom were then current. Saint Margaret was especially invoked in cases of pregnancy or demonic possession. Another aspect of Margaret's legend is, however, fascinating. The story goes that she entered a monastery, disguised as a man—one of many such legends that were circulating at the time.[41]

Whatever the reasons may have been, Joan eventually arrived at Chinon, the court of Charles, uncrowned king of France. Another mystery surrounds the events of this meeting between the king and Joan, but the results were plain to all. The French army rallied, the siege of Orleans was raised, there followed a string of military successes throughout April, May, and June of 1429, and finally Charles entered Rheims gloriously and was crowned king on July 17. A contemporary description of Joan during this period has come down to us: "The Maid, arrayed in white armor, rode on horseback before the King, with her standard unfurled. When not in armor, she kept state as knight and dressed as one. Her shoes were tied with laces to her feet, her hose and doublet were shapely, a hat was on her head. She wore very handsome attire of cloth of gold and silk, noticeably trimmed with fur."[42] This description is of the seventeen-year-old Joan, fast becoming a symbol of France to all her followers.

The legends were growing fast, many based on actual events. The story of the defeat of the English at Les Tourelles by Joan and her men was one of the most influential. Joan had been wounded by an arrow in the neck, but ignored her wound, rallied the men, and added to her legend the notion that she was invincible. It was all the more incredible, then, when the defeats started, and her capture the following May (1430) left the country in mourning. Prayers were publicly offered for her safety; one went as follows: "Almighty and Everlasting God, Who . . . hast ordained the coming of a young girl for the glory and preservation of the realms of France and also to repel and confound and destroy the enemies of the Kingdom, and Who has allowed . . . that she be imprisoned by the enemy, grant us . . . that she may be delivered from their power without suffering any hurt. . . ."[43]

Joan was captured by the English at Compiegne in May, and the following November was handed over to Bishop Cauchon who, for six months, had been preparing for her trial. Two months later, in January, 1431, the trial began at Rouen castle. There were over fifty sessions in all, at first public, then in the privacy of her cell. The charges were vague and often the questions were deliberately set to lure Joan into a trap. Her judges were bishops, lawyers, theologians well versed in the law. Joan was nineteen years of age, illiterate, and had no knowledge of the traps being set for her. Nevertheless, she confounded her inquisitors repeatedly. They floundered in her presence. Frequently, she refused outright to answer questions. Often her frustration and her spiritedness is shown in the answers. When being bullied about her voices and visions, one inquisitor asked her if Saint Margaret in her vision spoke English. "Why should she," snapped Joan, "when she is not on the English side." When pushed for answers about the dress of the Archangel Michael, another frequent source of her voices, Joan replied: "Do you think God has not the wherewithal to clothe him?"[44]

Whatever answer Joan gave was held in evidence against her. Of the final charges read to her, the fifty-first was that she had boasted that Saint Michael came to her. This was judged to be the height of rashness for a peasant woman, since no man "however upright, not even Our Lady, Mother of God, received such reverence or greeting."[45]

Throughout her trial, Joan was adamant on two points. She would not deny the existence of her voices nor that they came from God. And she would not change her male form of dress. At the end, there were five charges relating to her dress. But in the interrogation, Joan was as niggardly with information about the reasons for dressing thus as she was about everything else. Her only response was that "it was altogether necessary." Her clothes were connected in her mind with her mission, and she adamantly refused to change.[46] The appearance of a transvestite visionary must surely have confounded the inquisitors even further.

The bullying of the judges finally prevailed and Joan agreed to recant. On May 24, she was taken to a cemetery, placed on a scaffold and harrangued in front of an audience of French and English prelates and nobles from both countries. Again, the accounts are very confused. It seems that Joan who could not read or write was tricked into "signing" a recantation which she could not read and which had not been fully explained to her. Having signed, she seems to have changed to female clothing, but when she heard that she was not to be free, but was to spend the rest of her life in prison, Joan withdrew her recantation. The sign of her changed state of mind was the donning again of her male attire. Some historians are of the opinion that all this was a trick to make Joan into a lapsed heretic, for, as such, she could more easily be condemned to be burnt.[47] Whatever the case, that is in fact what happened. Here is another instance of a woman living the gospel, defined as it had been for centuries as manly virtue. Joan practiced virtue heroically the only way she knew—dressed as a man. And, as we saw, there were many Christian tales of saints who had done no less.

Joan went to the stake in Rouen on May 30, 1431. On her head she wore the criminal's cap with her crimes inscribed thereon—*Relapsed heretic, Apostate, Idolator.*[48] Later writers tell us that she went to her death crying the name of Jesus, that her half-burned body was exposed to the crowd so that, in prurient curiosity, they could see that she really was a woman, that then the pyre was rekindled and eventually her ashes were thrown in the Seine.

One is immediately struck by how friendless Joan is in the circle of the Church. There is no spiritual guidance available to her; all she receives is judgment and, in fact, trickery. No novelist could have dreamed up a character such as Joan—such a creation would seem outlandish. If Joan were to speak for herself about what characterized her life, she would doubtless point to her voices and her obligation to be obedient to them. Like Catherine, Joan seems to have bridged all classes. By not remaining in her allotted place in the structure, she made herself capable of speaking to all, at whatever level they found themselves. In return, the machinery of society and the Church turned on her. It was the prestigious University of Paris which had initiated her trial. At the time, there was great confusion about Joan's heresy.

One thing never really doubted about her was her virginity, despite the fact several examinations were judged necessary—even after her death. But virgins, and the power of virginity, were endowed with special sacrality in the Middle Ages.[49] A virgin heretic seemed incomprehensible. And so some of the greatest minds of the age had to resort to subterfuge to bring about Joan's downfall.

The impression which remains after exploring Joan's life is that of her absolute intransigence before her accusers. Before this monumental personal assurance, the judges floundered. "I refer myself to God and no other."[50] It is this massive assurance that left the Church with an uneasy conscience in Joan's case. Now that she was dead they were ready to reconsider the matter. As Marina Warner remarks, it is amazing how even Joan's admirers were much more comfortable with her dead than alive. Twenty years after the original verdict and the death of Joan, a process of nullifying the decision was begun. In 1456, the verdict of 1431 was rescinded.

In the intervening years the legend had grown, and finally in 1869, Monsigneur Dupanloup requested the Vatican to begin the proceedings for her canonization. The motives of patriotism and faith are difficult to distinguish during the process, but eventually Joan was canonized in 1920. The rehabilitation of Joan at her canonization included the naming of her judges in 1431 as schismatic. Joan appears in the calendar of saints as a "virgin." Her death did not apparently merit the title of martyr.[51]

What makes both Joan and Catherine so remarkable and so illuminating for our time is that they transcended the usual stereotype of female virtue. In this closing period of the twentieth century, these two women open up for us new visions of the unlimited potential of the Christian woman. They, like the other women we have seen, provide us with a quantum leap into a new dimension. The old patterns do not fit. The judges and theologians flounder. New possibilities seems possible and the light comes in the name of the voice. The notion of resistance is integral to Christian feminism and to all liberation theology. In Perpetua, Paula, Marcella, Catherine, and Joan we are presented with paradigms of resistance. Each of these women struggled towards her own liberation and full personhood in worlds even more hostile to such notions than our own. Each demonstrates a remarkable capacity for self-determination in societies and in a Church where their roles and positions were supposedly predetermined.

Each embodied the experience of liberation in her own life. And it was a religious experience. For each woman the context was different, the original inspiration was different, and the modality of living out the vision differed. But for each, the source was the all-encompassing will of God. Each did what she had to do without prior assurance of success. Each was indomitable in pursuing her vocation. Each woman was, for the most part, the initiator of her own life journey. Each knew herself to be called by God to do this task and no other.

Each refused to stay in her place.

Chapter 6

Carry Little Lanterns

Since the decline of the Middle Ages, the cry for reform had grown in Europe into a clamor of the people. Reform was demanded at all levels and for many different reasons. The word usually signified administrative and moral reform, and, as the word indicates, was backward-looking in its search for guidelines. When, in 1517, Martin Luther issued his famous doctrinal challenge at Wittenburg, there were few who could have seen that this was a significant moment in a series of events that would later be called the "Reformation."[1] Eventually, as we know, the diverse but united commonwealth that was medieval Christendom was shattered by this event. Here we do not intend to linger on the Reformation itself but on the subsequent efforts of the Catholic tradition to heal and renew the Church in "head and members."

The two women whose lives we shall explore in this chapter played significant roles in the movement for Catholic reform. Mary Ward's life was touched by the momentous change wrought in England by the religious crisis of the late sixteenth and seventeenth centuries.[2] Madame d'Houet did not begin her active role in the Church until the nineteenth century, but in many instances, the battles fought by Mary Ward had to be fought all over again by her nineteenth century sisters.[3] In each case, these women's lives were influenced by the fact that the Council of Trent did not provide for any direct participation by women in the mission of the Church. Both Mary Ward and Madame d'Houet felt called by God to precisely such a direct involvement.

The Council of Trent was the main instrument of the Roman Catholic reform. The most remarkable thing about it, as one historian has remarked, is that it was almost too late to deal with the divisions of Christendom.[4] Of all the complex results of this council, we choose to highlight only three. First, the council served to strengthen the position of the Pope; henceforth, Catholicism was to be controlled and directed from the center. Second, perhaps the most significant decision of the council was to direct bishops to open seminaries in their dioceses for the training of future priests. This decree not only hit at one of the major abuses in the Church—an ignorant clergy—but opened up the whole question of education. The third decision, which is of particular relevance here, was the decree making bishops responsible for the strict enclosure of all nuns in their respective areas. This one decree of the twenty-fifth session, dictated that henceforth there would be but one avenue open to women who wished to dedicate their lives to God, namely solemn vows lived out in an enclosed community.[5]

As the later history of the Catholic Church has so abundantly illustrated, it is precisely the work of active women religious in all areas of Catholic life which has contributed most to the Catholic reform at the level of the local Church. It is not necessary to delve into the complicated distinctions between nuns and sisters and women of the common life. The essential point is that the Council of Trent saw no place in the Church for the active apostolate of women and consigned them definitively, as it imagined, to the private sphere. It believed that a woman could do good to no one but herself, and, in fact, Mary Ward repeated this of herself at the beginning of her career when the road ahead was not clear.[6] The presupposition was that the work of renewing the Church was the work of men. No encouragement was given to women to engage in the public life of the Church; indeed this was actively discouraged and forbidden. Women in public were a liability, an obstacle.

Following in the tradition of the "God-possessed" women whose lives we have already studied, Mary Ward and Madame d'Houet followed faithfully and courageously along another path that they believed was pointed out to them by God. It was only their enormous confidence in their God-given vocations that sustained them. Mary Ward faced the imprisonment and death which was so often part of the life of a recusant. Madame d'Houet faced the seemingly interminable and often ill-tempered counseling of a series of spiritual directors, who collectively seem to have been determined to dissuade her from the validity of her call.

Despite the decrees of the Council of Trent, the eventual blossoming of reform in the Church seems to have been something of a series of accidents. In a very real sense one could say that one such accident was the wounding of a young Spanish soldier at the siege of Pampluna, a soldier who became known to succeeding ages as Ignatius of Loyola, founder of the Company of Jesus. At the death of Ignatius there were about one thousand Jesuits, as the members of his company came to be known; five years later they numbered thirteen thousand.[7] This army of Jesuits constituted a new force in the life of the Church—men, many of them ordained priests, committed to education and vowed to obedience to the Pope. The old monastic life had been modified significantly to allow these new Catholic reformers maximum freedom of movement in order to accomplish the renewal of the Catholic world.

The use of religious orders to reform the Church was not new. The glory of the Cluniac reform could still motivate Church leaders.[8] Most previous reform movements had proceeded by recalling the Orders to their primitive fervor. Now a new religious group, equipped with more members, more freedom of movement, more urgency, and more direction appeared to preside over the renewal of the post-reformation Church. One of the hallmarks of Jesuit life was the vow and spirit of obedience, and the concept of "obedience to the will of God" began to take on a particularity which had never before been part of the concept.

This presented a particular difficulty for women, a difficulty which added not a little to the sufferings of the two women whose lives are here considered. Obedience to the Church could only mean, for women, exclusion from the active apostolate of the Church. As in all previous ages of the Church, these women were able to articulate their vocation in terms of a higher obedience, which in the course of time was recognized by the Church.[9] It was

91

the tenacity, genius, and sanctity of the few women who attempted this hazardous journey which can truly be seen as responsible for the present inclusion of women in the Church. Women are by no means fully included as yet in the mission of the Church. There are women pioneers today who face as many hazards as their earlier sisters. The first skirmishes of the struggle in the modern Church are, however, instructive. Having searched throughout this book for new models and new visions of possibility for women in today's Church, we can rediscover some of the courage and confidence needed for the road ahead in the lives of Mary Ward and Marie Madeleine d'Houet.

Mary Ward

The life of Mary Ward was situated in one of the momentous periods in the history of England. She was born in Yorkshire in 1585 to a family of Catholic landowners still faithful to the "old religion" in the second generation of the Reformation in England. The same decade saw the deaths of two outstanding Catholics— Edmund Campion, the Jesuit, and Margaret Clitheroe, the housewife accused of harboring priests. Mary grew up amid tales of heroism and persecution, and among her relatives was able to hear at first hand the tales of prison life.[10] Mary's family was not atypical and was part of a network of rural gentry whose efforts did more than anything else to preserve and lend a special character to the Catholic life of the North of England.

Catholicism was being persecuted in England mainly for **political** reasons tied into the claims of Catholic and Protestant kings, emperors, Popes, and bishops. The Catholics of England were, for the most part, resisting for **religious** reasons, but were constantly under suspicion as traitors in league with Catholic Spain or papist armies. The excommunication of Elizabeth in 1570 by Paul III had made every English Catholic a traitor to the Crown.[11] The Catholic landowner provided a focus for resistance. In their rural homes were recreated the house churches of the early years of Christianity, and in many ways the landowner played the part of a bishop. It was the local leading family who dealt with the local authorities, who arranged for the visits of priests, who provided shelter for these same priests, who paid the fines for sheltering them and for not attending the "new" services, and who provided continuity of Catholic life to the surrounding community.

It was a life of constant tension, governed by a well organized network with links to the Catholic countries of the Continent. It had systems of codes, hiding places, lookouts, and disguises. We know too, from several sources, that it was a life of joy, and the stories of the heroes of this period, and indeed of Mary's own life, are filled with remarkable good humor and cheerfulness. They had learned how to "foil their enemies with joy."[12]

A time of persecution adds a new quality of self consciousness to religious life. A new religious spirit is born, a spirit kept alive by a constantly renewed commitment. A greater consciousness of time prevails. Each moment may be the last and so each moment is consciously offered to God. If each day is lived in this way, then each will be ready to respond with courage and cheerfulness when the dreaded knock comes announcing the arrival of the local authorities. The Mass, under the circumstances, was a rare privilege and, as a result, Eucharistic devotion came to be the focus of the spiritual life. Laws forbade the education of the next generation in the old faith but were certainly not obeyed in the Ward household. A whole series of Jesuit priests enjoyed the hospitality of the network of local houses, and Mary seems to have been excellently tutored in both religious and classical subjects.

As happened so often previously in the lives of Christian women, the crisis for Mary came with an arranged marriage. She resisted strenuously, and finally her family agreed to allow her to pursue her vocation. This entailed leaving England—itself a hazardous enterprise—and for the next several years Mary lived in St. Omer, then part of the Spanish Netherlands. This was the destination of many a young English "lady." After various attempts by well-meaning spiritual directors to ally her with one or other of the convents, Mary finally founded her own convent for English-speaking girls. Being part of the English nobility facilitated her entrance to the houses of the local bishops and nobles, and money seems at this time not to have been a problem. By 1608, the new convent was beginning to flourish, but Mary herself was more and more convinced that her own future lay elsewhere.

There followed journeys back and forth between England and St. Omer, where, eventually, Mary and a group of companions settled down to wait for God's will to be revealed. In the meantime education of the considerable numbers of English girls kept them fully occupied. Unceasing efforts were made to coax them to join one of the existing convents. Mary always listened respectfully, but her own insight and assurance that there would be another direction for her prevented any premature capitulation to the wishes of others.

Eventually a revelation of her future gave her the vision and the determination which was to mark the remainder of her life. In prayer she heard the words: "Take the same of the society."[13] Seemingly mysterious, it was crystal clear to Mary. She interpreted the words to mean that, as women, she and her companions were to engage in the same tasks as the Jesuits. This included the tasks of education and pastoral care, the right to live as vowed religious, and the freedom of movement as women that had been granted to the Jesuits. Eventually, Mary also stipulated that her group should be governed by one of their own women who would be directly responsible to the Pope. All of this, as has been seen, contravened the decrees of the Council of Trent. Such activity and such freedom was unheard of for women.

The remainder of Mary's life was engaged in making this vision a reality. It is a story of momentary successes and never-ending failures, charges and counter-charges, attacks from the Jesuits who were unwilling to have a female branch masquerading as Jesuitesses, and opposition from Church officials who could not envision that women should so self-confidently take on a public role in the mission of the Church.

Nevertheless, over all, the new group prospered. New houses were founded in Liège, Cologne, and Trèves.[14] The group gathered new friends both political and priestly who saw the value of their work and who recognized the integrity and veracity of Mary's vocation. Their apostolate grew to include prison visitation and work with the poor. In the uneasy religious atmosphere of the times, the "English Ladies" were often to run afoul of the law. These however, were but minor stresses compared to the overarching problem of gaining recognition for her new community. In the long run, her greatest trials and humiliations came from the leaders of the Church. Her request seemed simple enough, namely that the Church "should recognize once more that women could be trusted to do active work for God and yet be consecrated to Him." And further, that they be allowed to do this alongside the orders of men, but not subject to them.[15]

A "Memorial" was prepared by Mary for presentation to Pope Paul V, and one can trace there her sense of continuity with Christian women through the ages. She writes: "We propose to follow a mixed kind of life, such as we hold Christ Our Lord and Master to have taught his disciples, such a life as His Blessed Mother seems to have lived and to have left to those following her, such a life as appears to have been led by Saints Mary Magdalene, Martha, Praxedes, Prudentiana, Thecla, Cecelia, Lucy, and many other virgins and widows; and this most especially in these times in which, as in the early times of Christianity, the Church is sorely oppressed in our country. . . ." She continues with her request for permission to instruct young girls in "piety, Christian morals and the liberal arts."[16]

The Memorial was forwarded to Rome by a supportive bishop and reached Rome in 1616. An initially favorable reply gave their work added impetus. It was declared that further study was needed to be done before final approbation could be given.

Opposition to this final approbation seemed to come from all sides—from within her own ranks, from the Jesuits, from secular English priests, and from many bishops and cardinals—all of whom spied on her and her sisters continually. An opposition dossier of monumental proportions was being assembled based on gossip, inuendo, distorted reports of her "disobedience," and downright lies. When Mary decided in 1621 to go to Rome for a personal interview with the Pope she was probably unaware of the extent and ferocity of this opposition.

Accompanied by her first companions and some friends, Mary set out on foot for Rome, and was to spend a good part of the rest of her life in this fashion, journeying from place to place in search of support and in support of her scattered sisters. Again, she was greeted favorably by the Pope, now Gregory XV, but the opposition had already mounted a barrage of charges. The papal court, at this time, was the battleground where the Jesuits and the secular English clergy fought for the soul of the English Catholic Church. The Jesuits were extremely well organized; the secular clergy, scattered by persecution and lacking bishops, were not. The English priests easily interpreted Mary and her sisters to be dupes and tools of the Jesuits, intending to undermine further

95

their position in England. Gradually the whole of Rome turned against her, and a new Pope, Urban VIII seems to have listened more readily to charges that she was a "false visionary" and a "runaway nun."[17] By 1628, an order had been issued, without Mary's knowledge, to all bishops that the houses of the "English Ladies" were to be closed and their occupants scattered to their respective homes. By 1631, Mary Ward and her closest friend, Winefrid Wigmore were imprisoned, Mary herself being accused by the Inquisition as "heretic, schismatic and a rebel to the Holy Church."[18]

Mary was imprisoned with the Poor Clare sisters in their convent just outside Munich, there to be held incommunicado, constantly under guard and without the ministrations of the Church for Mass or sacraments. Her remarkable spirit seems never to have wavered. Indeed it was in this moment of defeat that her spirit of fun and irrepressible good humor seemed to have prevailed. Her early years in a recusant household were not in vain. She had learned the art of foiling her enemies with joy and a good deal of subterfuge. Even across the centuries her chuckles can be heard. Mary asked for lemons and corresponded with her sisters on scraps of paper, writing with lemon juice, which remained invisible until heated. She also devised a delightful system of code words, knowing how often in the past her letters had been stolen in transit. The "Jerusalems" were her opponents, her friends and associates were Ned, Will, Peter. She herself was called Felice, "the happy one," or "the old woman." Their hopes for reopening their houses were described as "setting up the loom again," when sufficient "yellow silk" (money) was available. In these letters, even Jesus himself had a code name—"Blue Lady's Son."[19]

Despite her efforts, the final Bull of Suppression was issued in 1631. It was declared that "certain women, taking the name of Jesuitesses, assembled and living together, built colleges and appointed superiors and a general, assumed a particular habit without the approbation of the Holy See . . . carried out works by no means suiting the weakness of their sex, womanly modesty, virginal purity . . . works which men most experienced in the knowledge of the Sacred Scriptures undertake with difficulty, and not without great caution. . . . "There are a number of remarks about contumacy and finally it is declared that the Institute is "suppressed, extinct and abolished."[20] One wonders if the men mouthing and writing these pomposities ever considered the inner contradictions of their writings, or ever noticed the courage, virtue, and godlikeness of the women they thus so easily dismissed.

Despite these fulminations, the work continued in a spasmodic, though no longer public way. Groups of friends such as Mary's followers were not so easily disbanded. Mary had returned to England, and the continued distress of the country provided in this instance a home where they could be safe from further persecution. Mary Ward died in 1645 on her native soil, still surrounded by her friends. Finally, in 1877, the work for which she had struggled with such courage and good cheer came to public recognition when the Institute of the Blessed Virgin Mary was allowed to claim her as their Founder.[21]

It remains for us to look briefly at the life of this remarkable woman, precisely as woman. The title of this chapter, Carry Little Lanterns, comes from the writings of a contemporary of Mary Ward's, one who fought similar battles in the tradition of the Ursulines. Her name is Anne de Xaintconge, and she wrote as follows:

> Our condition as women, as well as our defects, prevent us doing the work in the way that men do. . . It is forbidden us to aspire to their achievement, and we do not even think of it. But we have talents and capabilities as women, and it is not forbidden for us to use them to draw those of our own sex to religious life and to teach them what they are able for. . . We might not carry great flaming torches which cast the brilliant light of day on the Church; but we shall carry little lanterns instead, which will light up the hearts of young girls, servant maids, poor people and women.[22]

Despite their claim to be carrying little lanterns, the lives of many seventeenth century women opened the doors to the future of the Church. Mary, Anne, Chantal, Louise, and many others felt that they were called by God to work actively in the mission of the Church.[23] Nevertheless, they experienced this call in the context of the image of women traditionally held by the Church—the great work is done by men, women do the auxiliary work, not as important and not as glorious. Ministry to women was seen as one of these auxiliary tasks. In spite of this, it was a call to the frontiers of the Church's life because ministry to women had been

97

almost totally neglected in the life of the Church. The imposition of cloister symbolized the Church's thinking of the place of women in the life of the Church—"neither seen nor heard." Mary Ward and her companions, though they might not have been entirely conscious of the radical nature of their enterprise were intent on changing centuries of ingrained attitudes. Their shock at the continued opposition they met testifies to their lack of awareness that they were indeed revolutionaries.

Mary Ward did, however, perceive that a new kind of woman was needed for this new work—one who could combine sanctity with a great inner freedom. She wanted women who could move out into society and devote their full energies to the work of the apostolate. This notion of free women appeared frequently in her writings, and though it obviously did not carry the same meaning as it would today, nevertheless, the restrictions against which she labored were not so dissimilar to those of the late twentieth century.

Mary Ward worked on several drafts of a plan of life to facilitate this womanly freedom. Though her emphasis was always on the education of young girls, her sisters were encouraged to be ready to take on "any work whatever." This was the work of a woman with her eyes on the future. She was not asking for niggardly permissions; but she was sketching the future of woman's work in the Church. One work which she mentions specifically shows the scope of her vision. In the post-Reformation Church, where polarization seemed to have become the accepted state of affairs, Mary Ward asked her followers to be ready "to help in reconciling those estranged from the Church."[24] To further her plans for her followers, she realized only too well that the structures of traditional religious life for women would have to be greatly modified. Cloister would be a hindrance to the "mixed kind of life" she was recommending for her sisters. It is obvious that her early experience in a recusant household had enlarged her vision of what was possible for women in the Church. In a persecuted Church, the usual roles and restrictions break down. In England—as indeed in many other countries—it was the women and men householders in families like the Wards which provided the continuity of the Catholic tradition.

Her vision had developed considerably from her early years in religious life when that tradition indicated to her that a woman could do no good to anyone but herself. The intention of religious life for women was to provide the second redemption needed by them from the evil of their own carnality. This task would occupy all their energies. It seems to have been the report of a chance remark by a Jesuit which unleashed Mary's insight about the possible roles of women. The remark implied that women begin their enterprises with great fervor, but this soon pales because they are "mere women." The reporting of this remark caused great distress to the sisters and Mary delivered a series of "homilies" in order to rebut the implied accusation.

> There is no such difference between men and women that women may not do great things, as we have seen by the example of many saints. And I hope to God it will be seen that women in time to come will do much. . . . If women were made so inferior to men in all things, why were they not exempted in all things as they are in some? . . . As if we were in all things inferior to some other being which I suppose to be a man! Which I dare be bold to say is a lie; and with respect to the good Father may say it is an error.[25]

The Church of the seventeenth century was not ready to receive such strong service from its women members. The fact that "Jesuitesses" were setting out to convert England seemed an abomination. The women were accused of speaking on spiritual matters even in the presence of priests. They acted, it was said, "like preacheresses and teachers," instructing the people and calling them to repentance. They even taught contemplation to ordinary people. Such activities were not becoming to the "modesty" of women.[26]

It is obvious that Mary Ward and her sisters were not in any sense attempting to invade the realms of the ordained clergy. They simply wanted to engage in a ministry which was not being done. What is most impressive in all of this is Mary Ward's assurance of the rightness of her vocation, and the enormous amount of energy entailed in attempting to clear her own name and get her Institute recognized. "Masculine prejudice, traditionalist ideas, and inadequate understanding of the needs of the Church in the northern countries, together combined to create a situation which convicted the foundress of obduracy and willful disobedience."[27]

It is all the more remarkable that she died without bitterness, still urging her sisters forward to the "practice of God's vocation in us."[28] Women in today's Church owe it to her to continue the spirit which proclaimed: "I hope to God it will be seen that women in time to come will do much."[29] The ability of women to be founders, leaders, initiators, or pioneers has been unwillingly conceded by the Church at every period in history. This is as true in our own day as it was in Mary Ward's. It was no less true of the nineteenth century, a century which, like the seventeenth, saw a new stirring among women in the Church and a new flowering of communities for women. Among these was the community of Marie Madeleine d'Houet, the Sisters Faithful Companions of Jesus.[30]

Marie Madeleine d'Houet

The life of Marie Madeleine resembles that of Mary Ward in many ways, though she had probably never heard of her seventeenth-century sister. The followers of both women were referred to disparagingly as "Jesuitesses." Even more important is the tenacity which characterized both women—and indeed many other women founders—in adhering to their own God-given vision of the work required of them.

Marie Madeleine was born at Chateauroux, at the midpoint of France, in 1781. Despite the shadow of the Revolution, her childhood was happy, and both parents were committed to the faith then so much endangered in France. At twenty-three, she married Joseph de Bonnault d'Houet, a man of similar background. Together they ministered to typhus victims in the local hospitals. After less than a year of marriage, he was dead from the same typhus. A few weeks later, their son, Eugène was born, in September, 1805. After a few brief months of happiness, her life seemed devoid of all meaning except for the care of her infant son for whom "she would have laid down a thousand lives."[31] Her attention centered on him for the next six years, but gradually she began to pick up the threads of her former life of community service.

This time, however, she did not find there the same peace. Whether she cared for the sick or provided food for prisoners of war, there was a growing conviction within her that her true life's work lay elsewhere. Her nine-year old son had been registered at a Jesuit college in Amiens and there, as she says herself, she too discovered guidance for her life from the Jesuits. It was not to be simple.

There followed years of search, sometimes helped, sometimes hindered, by these same directors. It is frustrating, even today, to read the accounts of this period. Madame d'Houet, as she was widely known, came by degrees to the firm conviction that she was called to a new kind of life in the Church. Her Jesuit directors believed this too but seem to have fluctuated with astonishing swiftness from almost dictatorial conviction to helpless bafflement.[32]

It was a period of life paralleled in the life of many founders. Each woman felt convinced about the new directions of her work. Each director seemed convinced that it would fit under one of the already time-honored patterns for women's work in the Church. One fairly happy period of Mme. d'Houet's life resembled a similar period in Mary Ward's. Her home, now at Bourges, became a place of shelter for the Jesuits of antiroyalist and anticlerical France.[33] Here, in nineteenth century France, another house church led by a woman carries on the tradition of faith from the early Church, fourth-century Rome, and seventeenth-century Yorkshire.

Some aspects of her new work were becoming increasingly clear—she would found a society of women for the education of young children, for retreat work and for the missions—and she would do all this as a *une Jesuite*.[34] Like Mary Ward, this term spelled out for her a life of public active work as women in the Church combined with a strong spiritual life. In struggling towards the realization of her vocation, the women of the Gospels, the women around Jesus, began to provide for her inspiration and strength. Sometimes, like Mary of Bethany, she sat waiting at the feet of Jesus; sometimes, like the strong women who remained close to Jesus during the climactic events of death and resurrection, she felt endowed with renewed energy. Sometimes, like her namesake, Mary Magdalene, she felt empowered to go and tell the Good News to a starving nation.

The ambivalence of her Jesuit spiritual directors turned to active hostility when Mme. d'Houet announced that she had received guidance from God about the name of her new group— they would be called "Faithful Companions of Jesus." She writes of this: "It is not in their company (i.e. the Jesuits) that we are to walk but in that of Jesus Christ. . . . The divine Savior received women into his company and they accompanied him to the end. . . . Despite the love of John and the repentance of Peter, the women were first at the tomb and deserved to see the Risen Jesus first."[35]

Finally her work began at Amiens in 1820. Two companions had joined her and they "borrowed" seven poor children from the local convent of the Sisters of Charity. From this small beginning when Marie Madeleine was thirty-eight grew a Society that before her death was to number hundreds of members in twenty-five convents in France, Italy, Switzerland, Ireland, and England. Their work centered on the education of young children, but also included evening classes for factory workers and the catechesis of adult women. The convents, as well as being places of prayer, work, and teaching, were also offered on Sundays as places of recreation to poor women and children.

The life and formation of the Sisters, though based on the Jesuit rule, were stamped with Mme. d'Houet's own genius. The guiding spirit was not any Jesuit, but the life of Jesus in the Gospels. Her writings testify to her strong love for the gospel women, and though at first she seemed called to be *une Jesuite*, her inspiration was soon based on Mary Magdalene and the women companions of Jesus. This was what the name of her community meant to her—they were to be followers of Jesus. This name was to cost her a great deal of anguish, but she would not accept any alternative.

The time had come by 1826 for Mme. d'Houet to go to Rome to ask for the approval of her little group. As this became known, the Jesuit harassment which had plagued her thus far turned into determined opposition. Pope Leo XII, however, assured her that she no longer need to follow Jesuit direction, and formally confirmed the name of Faithful Companions of Jesus.[36] Final approbation of the Society would follow in due course. By 1837, since there had been no further word for eleven years, Mme. d'Houet set off again for Rome in search of full and final approbation for her Society. This time, under Jesuit influence, all doors were closed to her. Pope Gregory XVI refused to see her and was reported to be "exceedingly displeased." This time the cries of heretic were not heard as in the seventeenth century, but Mme. d'Houet and her companions were denounced as "restless and scheming personages."[37] All their former friends in Rome treated them with cold indifference. This response left her plagued with doubts about her whole enterprise. On an inspiration, she prepared another petition, this time sending it directly to the Pope. Eventually, they were summoned to an audience, and the final approbation was cordially given on August 5, 1837.[38]

Despite this, her opponents continued their harassment and over the next few years managed to have several of her houses suppressed. At times she feared, as bishop after bishop turned against her, that the Society was on the brink of dissolution. It is hard to pinpoint the reasons for this opposition. The available sources seem to suggest Jesuit interference on all fronts, but there are no specific charges of a canonical or doctrinal nature. One can only conclude that masculine prejudice was as strong in that age as in the previous—and present one. One cannot help wondering why women's work within the Church provoked such mighty opposition, especially since, as in the case of these two women, every attempt was made to secure all the necessary ecclesiastical approbations. The journey from following to leading in the Church, is for women, fraught with a great deal of frustration.

Mme. d'Houet died on April 5, 1858, and her remains, after being interred at Gentilly until 1904 and at Birkenhead until 1980, now rest at the Motherhouse in Broadstairs, Kent, in the south of England.[39] Since her death, the work of the Sisters Faithful Companions of Jesus has spread into four of the five continents and still centers around educational, retreat, and mission work, according to the needs of the Church of the twentieth century.

Despite the heroic efforts of the reforming women of the seventeenth century, the task of assuming a place in the public mission of the Church was still surrounded with difficulties in the nineteenth century. Today, women in religious communities, who, in the spirit of their sisters at all ages in the history of the Church, reach out to new challenges and new frontiers, often face similar opposition. Newness in the Church's mission has so often been in the hands of women. The consequent disapproval has always been phrased in substantially the same language—the women are "gadabouts," novelty-seekers, "disobedient" or "bitchy, brittle feminists." We owe a great debt of gratitude to all these women who kept alive and provided models for women of full inclusion in the mission of the Church, following no masculine stereotypes, but a life based on taking up the agenda of Jesus in the Gospels. These women showed in their lives shrewdness, humility, and obedience, but not subservience. Their lives were dictated by a "higher obedience," and to Magdalene, Perpetua, Paula, Marcella, Joan, and Catherine, we can now add Mary and Marie Madeleine and a host of others.

Chapter 7

The Church Teaches

What does the Church teach about women? For most people, for most women, this question has probably never been raised to consciousness, never been articulated. The presumption is that the Church teaches generally that all are God's children and that all who are baptized are full members of the Church—women, too. The one-sided image of the Church presented to us—all male ministers and a female majority of active members—is explained in various ways, but the common assumption often is that a woman can do any good work she wants in the Church. Most women, it is assumed, have been happily engaged in doing what they have to do. The few who wanted to pursue their vocations have some options open to them—what more could be needed? This happy picture is often shattered when young girls or women try to act on the assumption that they are full members of the Church and take what they feel to be their roles in its life. The shock of resistance is still the greatest awakener of women to the ambivalence and negativity of the Church towards their status. The lives of the great women of history demonstrate that the place of women in the Church has always appeared differently to women who tried to follow out their vocation than to the male leaders who presumed that they knew "women's place in the Church."

This chapter will explore some of the accumulated teaching of the Church about women. Before the context of the teaching is examined, one obvious point needs to be made—all the teachers are male, all the teachers are clergy, and all the teachers are celibate. Having respectfully acknowledged the integrity of most of the individual males, their guidance by the Holy Spirit in their roles as leaders, and their intention for the good of the Church, it nevertheless remains true that the teaching of the Church about women means what ordained celibate males have taught about women. Women themselves have never been consulted or deemed worthy of consultation about their relationship with God or the Church. Five chapters of this book have explored the lives of strong, active, saintly, God-possessed women in the life of the Church. No one of them, nor indeed any other woman, has ever been an active member of the official teaching Church. Even the most casual observer will be prepared for a one-sided view of women based on the one-sided questions asked and the one-sided experience brought to the theological reflection. Even the most casual observer recognizes that neither humanity nor the Church is comprised only of males. With this in mind we will be prepared for the particularly one-sided teaching of the Church on the role of women.

We have chosen a few moments throughout history as our main point of focus—the Pauline teaching in the early Church, patristic teaching in the fourth and fifth centuries, the teaching of Thomas Aquinas in the Middle Ages, and the teaching of some twentieth century bishops and Popes. These writings, though scattered through different periods, cultures, and political moments in the life of the Church, nevertheless exhibit remarkable similarities and consistencies.

Pauline Teaching

First then to the Pauline teaching. The adjective *Pauline* is used here to refer to the epistolary segment of the New Testament traditionally acknowledged as Pauline. Even though distinctions are made today about the authorship of these letters, they have functioned in the Church, particularly in regard to their teaching on women, as coming from the hand or at least the mind of Paul.[1] The one word that can be used to describe the attitude of Paul towards women in his authentic letters is *ambivalent*. In the post-Pauline literature, this ambivalence is not noticeable, and a more consistent negative evaluation of women is present.

The charter of Christianity is given in the letter to the Galatians: "For as many of you as were baptized into Christ have put on Christ. There is neither Jew nor Greek, there is neither slave nor free, there is neither male nor female; for you are all one in Christ Jesus."[2] This vision of an inclusive community of coequal disciples was the force behind the missionary work of the earliest decades of Christianity. Women and men collaborated in the mission of the Church as partners, as has been shown.[3] Eventually, however, questions were asked and distinctions began to be made. The world within which the first century Church took root was a patriarchal world, a man's world. The public sphere was a man's place, the private sphere was woman's. Between Jewish tradition and Hellenistic tradition there were some differences, though in general they were but a matter of degree. It was not traditional Judaism running up against a more liberal Hellenism which caused friction in the early Church, but the gospel vision of equality running up against a patriarchal structure which was all-pervasive.

Initially the questions seemed innocent enough—questions about the ordering of worship, about different customs of women's dress in public gatherings, questions about family relationships and the ordering of family life.[4] These questions in fact would not have arisen had Christianity not been a community with a new vision of the equality of its members. Women and men did not congregate together in the ancient world of either Judaism or Hellenism. When faced with these questions in the particular context of the Corinthian community, Paul's contribution was to doubt the power of the Christian vision to sustain these differences.

When faced with questions about the role of women in the Churches, Paul, while acknowledging the equality of discipleship wrought by baptism, nevertheless, chose as his basic premise the inequality of the prevailing social structure of patriarchy. He moved from the promise of the vision of Jesus to a compromise. The compromise consisted in not having sufficient faith in the vision of Jesus but in "baptizing" instead the structures of patriarchy. What emerged was a kind of "love patriarchalism." We are familiar with the ensuing commands: "the women should keep silent in the churches," "If there is anything they desire to know, let them ask their husbands at home," "It is not good for a man to touch a woman," "The wife does not rule over her own body, but the husband does," "The head of every man is Christ, the head of a woman is her husband, and the head of Christ is God. . . . For a man ought not to cover his head since he is the image and glory of God; but woman is the glory of man. (For man was not made from woman but woman from man.)" "Wives, be subject to your husband as to the Lord."[5] And in the Pastorals: "Women should adorn themselves modestly and sensibly in seemly apparel, not with braided hair or gold or pearls or costly attire," "Let a woman learn in silence with all submissiveness. I permit no women to teach or to have authority over man; she is to keep silent. For Adam was formed first, then Eve; and Adam was not deceived, but the woman was deceived and became a transgressor. Yet woman will be saved through bearing children."[6]

Only the earlier quotations listed here are genuinely Pauline; the latter, especially those from the Pastorals come from several decades later in the life of the Church. The spirit and intent of both is the same, however, and most importantly for our purpose, have been used as authoritative Pauline teaching throughout most of the Church's history. The attitude of exclusiveness is immediately obvious. Women were removed from collaboration to almost complete passitivity by no greater a claim than Paul's lame conclusion, "Anyway we have no other custom."[7] Unless notice is specifically given to the contrary in all Church documents the word "we" is to be interpreted as "we males."

Paul's compromise was in opting for the societal structures based on the household codes which were common in the ancient world. They functioned, in a sense, as manuals of etiquette, and detailed all manner of relationships in private and public life—relationships between masters and slaves, husbands and wives, fathers and children. Paul took these codes and converted them to Christian use by introducing expressions such as "in the Lord" or "as to the Lord."[8] In this way a series of social structures which treated women as inferior to males and of less value were consecrated as Christian practice. And not only were they to be practiced by Christians, they were to be seen as the expression of God's will. For the first time, patriarchal structures were given a Christian theological base. The theological rationale was rooted in the second creation story where Eve is created from Adam's rib and especially in the story of the Fall.[9] This was a completely new interpretation of the role of Eve—she had never before been seen as a model for expressing God's will in regard to women. Eve sinned first, her punishment was childbearing and submission to her husband. This was then expanded to include, as an expression of the divine will, the subjection of all women to all men.

Though later we will study some papal teaching in more detail, this is an appropriate place to examine some other passages of the homily to newly married couples given by Pope Pius XII and quoted in chapter 1. The Pope began his homily by commenting on the wife and husband as "ministers of the great sacrament," stating his awareness that, as such, they were acting "on a perfectly equal footing." Both entered into the "contract of matrimony" with "full independence" and as persons "absolutely equal." He continued: "But in that same moment you founded a society; every family is a society; every well ordered society needs a head; every power of headship comes from God. . . ." The male was acknowledged as the head for the following reason: "he was the first to be formed, and afterwards Eve. And St. Paul said that it was not Adam who was deceived, but the woman. . . ." The Pope then jumped down the years to the group of women to whom he is speaking and seemed incapable of making distinctions between the mythical Eve and the real women to whom he speaks. The paragraph deserves quotation in full:

> Oh how much harm Eve's curiosity, in looking at the beautiful fruit of the earthly paradise and her conversation with the serpent, did to the first man, to Eve herself, to all her children, and to us! Besides multiplying her sorrows and sufferings, to her God said that she would be subject to her husband. O Christian wives and mothers, never be taken off guard by the desire to wield the scepter in the family. Let your scepter— the scepter of love—be that which the Apostle of the Gentiles places in your hands: to save yourself through child-bearing, if you continue in faith and love and sanctification with sobriety.[10]

The new vision of the divinely willed order of creation came to be of enormous fundamental significance to the life of the Church through the centuries. There is a place for women—at the bottom of a God-ordered hierarchy. This place is further to be specified by Church teachers, and the home or convent have been designated as the appropriate places for women to live their

Christian lives. It is obvious that since only men are teachers, the roles assigned to women in any particular age will be those perceived to be of most benefit to men. Women are to be taught, their roles are prescribed and proscribed, and this is true of both home and Church. It is, indeed, a foolproof theological structure, and has functioned effectively throughout history to keep women at the margins of Church leadership and Church decision-making, and, in spite of their numerically superior presence, at the margins of parish life.

The conclusion in Christian teaching is that the vision of equality offered by Jesus and perceived dimly by Paul is to be affirmed of our origins (we come equally from the hand of God), and of our destiny. Here below the social structures of patriarchy will be more influential for the ordering of our lives. Christianity has contributed, it is taught, by removing the harshness from these ancient codes, but the central premise of the inferiority and necessary submission of women remains the same.

It is immediately obvious that women through the centuries, while undeniably damaged by these struggles, have nevertheless managed on occasion to rise above them. The lives of all the women studied in this book followed "a higher obedience," but their lives were enormously hampered by the protestations of Church officials that women were constitutionally unable to do precisely what they were doing so well, namely to follow God's will in working publicly in the mission of the Church.

Patristic Teaching

We move now to patristic teaching on women and to one element in particular. The instructions of Paul had been well learned; by the fourth century, the official ministry of the Church excluded women almost universally. In this period, the focus of attention was on another of the dicta of Paul: "It is good for a man not to touch a woman."[11] For this was the period when the first great fragmentation of the Christian image occurred, the period of monasticism. The image of the perfect Christian in the fourth century was that of the female or male celibate whose life was devoted exclusively to God. We have seen how this call was capable of such great liberating power in the lives of women like Marcella. Now we must examine, too, the further degradation of the image of women by "Fathers" of the Church who considered "femaleness" in itself a sin.

When the monastic life for women in the West began to be legislated by men, it was not always the element of devoted following of the call of God which was emphasized, but the responsibility of women to redeem themselves a second time from the liability of their femaleness. Often in the writings of Jerome, Ambrose, Augustine, Chrysostom, and many others, one gets the impression that an ideal Church would be one composed entirely of celibates. Today it is hard to evaluate some of this writing other than humorously. The men are so patently misogynistic and seemingly so helpless in the face of their own sexuality. Their self-hatred was easily projected onto the perceived cause of all their personal unrest, namely the reality of femaleness.

By the fourth century, Christianity had become strongly dualistic in its orientation. What was holy was of the spirit. What was sinful was bodily. On the side of the holy were included the more rational and controlled and virtuous males, virtue being understood in terms of rationality and control. Sin originated in the material world, in the flesh, in the body. Women, Eve, were on this side of the dualist divide, supposedly sunk more deeply in the things of the flesh than were males. Besides they were more emotional, and less controlled. It was obvious that leadership belonged to the rational. Virginity for women was like a second redemption from their bodiliness. Virginity raised them to the level of males and opened for women the possibility of holiness.

The general spirit of much of the teaching is summed up in these sentences from John Chrysostom: "Woman is a foe to friendship, an inescapable punishment, a necessary evil. Among all the wild beasts there is not one that is more harmful than woman."[12] Similar quotations could be added in voluminous quantity from the writings of other "Fathers." That is neither helpful nor necessary. Much has been written both in defense of the patristic writers and in rage against them. The point to be made here is that their writing has become authoritative, if not in word, then certainly in spirit. Their contribution to the teaching about women in the Church was to focus attention on the woman as temptress. Virginity was seen for centuries as a better choice and a more holy way of life for both women and men. The choice of marriage, and the necessary subjection of women in marriage

111

which was fundamental to the Christian vision as taught by the Church, resulted in the closing down of the spiritual horizons of women for centuries.

The dangers of a one-sided and one-sexed teaching office in the Church is more than abundantly illustrated in the lives of the "Fathers". Their own unhealthy sexuality was blamed on the presence of women. Not only was the woman's point of view not considered necessary to the debate, women were not considered to have a point of view. They were receivers of teaching; their behavior was even further curtailed. An attitude of hatred of women was embedded in the Church, and the male defense of celibacy was, despite theoretical foundation, tainted throughout history by implied disrespect and often outright cruelty towards women.

The "Fathers" of the Church added significantly to the Church's teaching on the life of virginity and marriage. It is usually added in their defense that they did not disparage marriage.[13] From a woman's perspective, this defense can scarcely be made. Teaching consists of more than mere words. Teachers are responsible for the emotional wrapping of their teaching and for its on-going effects. The teaching of the "Fathers" of the Church has influenced centuries of prejudice against women, and any woman reading their fulminations will feel that all women have suffered sufficiently from their misogynistic dualism.

Thomas Aquinas

The wisdom and theology of Thomas Aquinas had been normative in the Church for centuries prior to the second Vatican Council. This was apparent not only in volumes of papal teaching but also in Canon Law, where it was stated that the study and teaching of rational philosophy and theology must follow exclusively the method, doctrine, and principles of the Angelic Doctor. This obviously applied also to his teaching on women, a great part of which has been proven wrong by modern science. The conclusions, which were based on these false premises, still prevail and still have an enormous influence on contemporary teaching on women. Thomas, not surprisingly, had little scientific understanding of the processes of reproduction. He added little to the theories of Aristotle, who suggested that, in the act of human generation, the male provides the active substance and is therefore superior. The role of the female is like that of a field. She receives the seed, in which the whole human "form" is present, and allows it to be nourished from her body. According to both Aristotle and Thomas, the normal result of every conception, then, would be a male human person. The birth of a female indicated that an accident had happened. Female persons were deviations from the norm, and Thomas guessed that dampness in the air or the direction of the wind at the time of conception made the difference.[14]

Thomas wrote, then, that as a result, the "father should be loved more than the mother." For the father "is principle in a more excellent way than the mother, because he is the active principle, while the mother is a passive and material principle."[15] Since the woman is thus passive, material (that is, not spiritual), receptive, and deviant, it can be presumed that the woman in Thomas' theology did not fare very well. Since women seemed to exist in large numbers, Thomas has to conclude that, though a woman was not intended in any single act of creation, women in general were intended by God to exist.[16] Thomas proceeded to draw moral conclusions from these premises about a woman's capabilities. A woman was base, defective, weak, and imperfect. As such, of necessity, she was to be in complete subjection to man. Following Paul, he pointed out that this natural subjection was confirmed by the divine curse on Eve and all her descendents.[17] When he looked for some reason to justify the existence of women at all, Thomas was of the opinion that childbearing, housekeeping, and being generally as helpful as possible to men provided adequate reasons. "Husband and wife are not equal in marriage, neither as regards the marriage act, in which the more noble part is that of the husband, nor as regards household management, in which the wife is ruled and the husband rules."[18] Thomas added further that "the image of God is found in the man, not the woman, for man is the beginning and end of woman, as God is the beginning and end of every creature."[19] As a woman, one can only respond to such arrogant theologizing with Mary Daly that "when God is male the male is God."

Thomas, nevertheless, was faced with the problem of the soul, which he taught is a direct creation of God. This meant then that the contribution of the male in the act of conception was as "material" as that of the female. One of his theological theories canceled out the other. Thomas never really faced this inner contradiction in his theology, nor did any of his later followers until very recently. Though Thomas did not spell it out, his theology of the direct creation of the soul by God would indicate that each and every person, women included, was intended and directly created by God, and in God's image. These conclusions were not made by Thomas.[20] Again it is easy to see the dangers to one half of humanity when all the official theologizing is done by the other half. Thomas can be forgiven his outdated information about reproduction. The male theologians who followed him down the ages cannot be as easily forgiven for continuing his conclusions about women even when his premise had been proven false.

It is hard to imagine today how a theologian such as Thomas, lauded through the centuries for his contributions to the understanding of the Christian mystery, could look out at his world and be blind to the existence, gifts, sanctity, and devotion to the Church of the other half of the human race. His blindness makes the claim of "objective" truth much more difficult to maintain in the Church. Thomistic theology was lauded for its excellent methodology in helping towards the "pure truth" of the Christian mystery. It was the perfect marriage of faith and reason. While granting the significant influence of Thomas on later theologians and on the Church's life, granting also his own sanctity and integrity, nevertheless, for women, the whole theological enterprise of the Angelic Doctor is vitiated by their degradation at his hands. And if for the women members of the Church, this is so, then it is also true of the whole Church. Even today, we still await the full rehabilitation of women as perfect, whole, human beings, created in the image of God.

The Twentieth Century

It is because of the authoritative nature of the teaching of Thomas that some feminist writers are calling ever more loudly for a new authoritative papal teaching restoring to women their full dignity as members of the Church. Many women today have already drawn this conclusion for themselves. The official teaching of the Church, however, even in twentieth century language, continues many of the principles of Thomas. One feminist has written:

> In order to lay to rest the theology of indirect redemption that has plagued the misunderstood humanity of women, it is time for the Church to speak plainly, boldly and clearly its acceptance of women as full human being. . . If the case can be made that one kind of human, the woman, is genetically inferior and disposed by nature to a state of subjugation, then domination is clearly part of the creative scheme. If women are less than men, so different as to be incompetent, so unreasonable as to be incapable, then it is a very short step to the justified napalming of Orientals, the lynching of blacks and the extermination of Indians because, it can be argued, the Creator God built inferiority right into the human race.

She then quoted some of the "great men of the Church" on the role of women, each as insulting as the other and concluded "So spoke the great men of the Church. . . . It is time for a Pope to speak otherwise."[21]

The role of women in the Church has, in fact, been a favorite topic of Popes and bishops in the twentieth century. Though many changes are evident in this writing, the longed-for encyclical on the full equality of women seems as far off as ever. Following is a brief selection of this papal and episcopal material in an effort to discern the official teaching in today's Church on the position of women.[22]

By way of introduction to this final section on the teaching of recent Popes and bishops on the roles and positions of women in the Church, we must say that almost every advance of women in the social sphere has been resisted more or less vigorously by the Church. This is so because each move forward enlarges the range of options for women in such a way that the completely home-bound woman is no longer the reality in today's world. The increasing participation of women in political, professional, industrial, athletic, and corporate life has not been without much hand-wringing in the Church. One might add that the recent euphoria about the selection of a woman United States vice-presidential running-mate signals that the move of women into the public sphere has taken another step forward.

Pope Pius XII had already warned of the dangers to women's "best interests" by this opening up of public life. He lamented the increasing interaction between women and men in the public sphere which has developed to such an extent that "husband and wife find themselves well-nigh in a position of equality." The fact of the increase in the family budget brought about by the work of women was another cause of distress to him. "Often they exercise professions of the same order, render to the family budget a contribution practically equal, while that same work leads them to live very independently of one another." The proper patriarchal structure cannot survive in this atmosphere. "Why wonder if in these circumstances the sense of hierarchy in the family fades and begins to disappear?" A woman's true place in the family was in submission, and the Pope mourned the passing of "iron discipline," thus allowing women to become "practically independent of the authority of the husband." He pointed out that love can make this subjection a sweet burden, and the subsequent relationship of inferiority sweetly borne shows the complementary natures of males and females at their best. Such were the "unchangeable duties of wives and mothers," and all dreams of "parity in studies, in school, in science, in sports, in competition" were to be treated as so many "lying, tempting, deceiving voices."[23]

A few years earlier the cause of all this unrest in the lives of women had been pinpointed by the cardinal archbishop of Boston as "sinister feminism." This is one of the earliest references to this "sinister" reality in modern Church documents, and there is no mistaking what the good cardinal thought of it: "The one thing that will preserve proper order in your house" he says, "is the Christian authority of the Christian father of a family. . . . There is no doubt that one of the main causes of this sinister feminism, of which we hear so much and read quite enough, is what would appear to be a growing weakness on the part of the manhood of the nation. . . The very fact that women are often clamoring to take all power and authority into their hands is certainly no compliment to the manhood of the Nation. . . ."[24]

This was written in the *New York World* in 1920. Five years previously, in 1915, Cardinal Gibbons of Baltimore attempted to put women back where they belonged—on a pedestal. Here again was heard the "best interests" of women. When men denied them the vote, women were to trust that the men had their best interests at heart. "The insistence on the right of participation in active political life is undoubtedly calculated to rob woman of all that is amiable and gentle, tender and attractive; to rob her of her grace of character and give her nothing in return but masculine boldness and effrontery."[25]

The cardinal continued to demonstrate that he too had the "best interests" of women at heart. "When I deprecate female suffrage I am pleading for the dignity of woman. I am contending for her honor, I am striving to perpetuate those peerless prerogatives inherent in her sex, those charms and graces which exalt womankind and make her the ornament and coveted companion of man. Woman is queen indeed, but her empire is the domestic kingdom."[26]

Despite such laments and warnings, women continued to seek educational, professional, and personal advantages for themselves, and, if married, for their families. Much of the distaste evident in Church documentation even today fails to take into account the fact that by far the majority of the poor are women, and that in Canada, for example, women earn only sixty percent of what men in comparable positions earn.[27] The move to the public sphere is not part of some "sinister" plot on the part of women: it is often a necessity of survival.

What of the post-Vatican II Church? In many ways the situation today resembles the Pauline ambivalence of the early Church. Side by side with ringing declarations of human rights and personal dignity, the same pedestalizing tendencies are to be found. Some things, however, have changed. The reality of the vast changes in cultural and political life entailing the presence of women in the public sphere is taken for granted. Document after document addresses this situation. All the post-Vatican II Popes recognize that women are actively engaged in all fields of human endeavor. Because of this very fact, though, they perceive a need to proclaim again the rights and dignity of women.[28]

On the other hand, the reality of all forms of discrimination is recognized, including sexual discrimination. "Among the victims of injustice—unfortunately no new phenomenon—must be placed those who are discriminated against in law or in fact, on account of their race, origin, color, culture, sex or religion."[29] The efforts of various countries to put an end to discrimination by legislation are noted with approval, and there are even some suggestions that such efforts may be made by the Church.

Pope Paul VI listed some of the rights of women which should be encouraged in any civilized society.[30] Among these are:

1. The recognition of the civil rights of women as the full equals of men, whenever these rights have not been acknowledged

2. Laws that will make it possible for women to fill the same professional, social, and political roles as men, according to the individual capacities of the person

3. The acknowledgment, respect, and protection of the special prerogatives of women in marriage, family, education, and society

4. The maintenance and defense of the dignity of women as persons: unmarried women, wives, and widows; and the help they need, especially when the husband is absent, disabled, or imprisoned, that is, when he cannot fulfill his function in the family

Other documents go on to express concern for the economic rights of women and for the improvement of their working conditions. However, the subject of working always brings up in Vatican documents the notion of the family as the proper place for women.[31] The notion that work other than housework is always exceptional in a woman's life prevails, even when demands are being made for proper working conditions.

The general amelioration of the position of women in society is at this stage of the twentieth century acknowledged in official papal writing as good and inevitable. Doubt continues to be expressed about the preservation of the true dignity of women in these different circumstances, and in this context the ancient teaching of Thomas takes on a new form. For, the documents uniformly insist that women have a "special nature," established by God, and that this should dictate the roles and relationships undertaken by them in society. This "special nature" of women grows primarily from her role as mother. This is what the female personality has that is essentially specific to it, in the words of Pope Paul VI. Woman's true vocation is to be mother.[32]

The closing message of Pope Paul at the Second Vatican Council addressed a series of special interest groups within the Church. His message to women, though already quoted, deserves to be repeated here. The Council addressed them thus: "You women have always had as your lot the protection of the home, the love of beginnings, and an understanding of cradles. You are present in the mystery of a life beginning. You offer consolation in the departure of death. Our technology runs the risk of becoming unhuman. Reconcile men with life and above all, we beseech you, watch carefully over the future of our race. Hold back the hand of man, who, in a moment of folly, might attempt to destroy human civilization."[33] As an aside, one might have thought that a direct appeal to such murderously inclined men might have been more to the point.

Vatican documents often spoke of "false equality," and here they do not venture very much beyond the position of Pope Pius XII. False equality seems to be any move that will take a woman away from her "proper vocation," any assumption of responsibilities other than those that can "rightfully be theirs," any work other than the "specific work proper to women."

As the Popes move closer to articulate women's "special role" of motherhood, the language becomes more and more poetic, and less specific. Women have the task of making the truth "sweet, tender and accessible" in daily life. Their special qualities of "intuition, creativity, sensibility, a sense of piety and compassion, a profound capacity for understanding and love" fit them especially for works of reconciliation in the family and society.[34] Not however in the Church!

The above listed qualitites make women especially suited for the work of evangelization, though the discussion of the far-reaching work of women in this area seems to apply only to women of religious congregations. It is also highly ambiguous. On the one hand, the "right and duty of all Christian people" by reason of their baptism to participate as fully as possible in the work of the Church is emphasized. On the other hand, the document *Ministeria Quaedam* stated: "In accordance with the venerable tradition of the Church, installation in the ministeries of lector and acolyte is reserved to men."[35] Women are encouraged to participate in ministry, but they must not be seen to do so officially.

There is evidence, then, of much development over the years in the official teaching of the Church about the roles of women. Their advancement in all aspects of society is greeted with approval. A similar enthusiasm is not evident about the roles of women in the Church. The main contribution of a woman here seems to be that of mother. The documents clearly assume a special understanding of the humanity of women, based on the essential characteristics of motherhood. It is only when speaking directly of motherhood that women can assume that the texts are in fact addressing them. At other times, even when speaking of "all the baptized," the writers seem to have only male Christians in mind.

Pauline, patristic, and Thomistic anthropology and theology are still present in the Church's teaching about the "specialness" of women. Women are rarely if ever treated as simply human without some qualification. One is left with the conclusion that women are not quite human, not quite members of the Church and not quite baptized. One is certainly left with the knowledge that women are not welcome in the official ministry of the Church.

One of the main difficulties of this official teaching and a continued problem in its interpretation is that women are treated as a group, as a sex. No allowances are made for differences among women. The papal writing, while acknowledging the social advances of women, does not avail itself of recent studies of women in psychology, anthropology, or theology. Even new insights in biblical studies have not yet been included in official teaching about women. The starting point seems still to be the Pauline and Thomistic view of a divinely ordered reality where all women, just by reason of their sex, have a special place. The notion of a complementarity of the sexes, with men again prescribing the "complementary" roles of women still takes precedence over a view of the complementarity of persons, where each individual person contributes freely of her or his own individual gifts. One writer comments: "Every human partnership of whatever kind, is based not on equality of gifts, but on a relationship of mutual trust that allows each to find his or her best forms of service and affirms this in others. To assume we know a person's gifts simply because of her or his biological sex is a form of 'heresy,' because the Spirit works in many ways through people."[36]

In conclusion, we can say that the Church still offers an ambivalent message to its women members. There is a recognition and condemnation of injustice, discrimination, and sexism in society, and support for all efforts to ameliorate the position of women wherever their dignity is threatened.

120

This forthright message does not seem to include the society of the Church. An image often used to illustrate the improvement of the condition of women in the Church is that of the "opening of doors." Some doors have been opened, but there is a clear message that they will open further only in what concerns the "special nature" of women. This indicates that the door to the ordination of women to the priesthood cannot be opened without enormous changes at many levels in the teaching of the Church.

No real progress can be made until a dialogue takes place with women. The voices of women are not heard in the Churches. Women have never been invited as equal partners in an eyeball-to-eyeball dialogue. The language of misogyny has died; the language of patriarchy has not. Women are addressed as a group, a special interest group, and not as individuals with gifts and religious experience, not, in a word, as persons. In being addressed as a group, they are also assured that a group response of obedience is all that is required of them. Differences of opinion among women are not expected. Hence the exasperation of many Church leaders when greeted with varied demands from women. A group response is expected. Womankind should speak with one voice. Women are addressed as "out there," over against the Church. The language of the documents indicates that the Church is speaking to women as if they were not a part of the Church.

While ambivalence is present in word, it disappears almost entirely in practice. Liturgical celebration in language, gesture, and leadership is not ambivalent about the position of women. The teaching in gesture is clear. Women are not equally present. They are not equal members. The Church speaks and celebrates as "brothers" and others.

The present Pope, John Paul II, shows no sign of changing this teaching. He does not seem to understand the significance of women's contribution to the Church. He gives no evidence of any need to hear what women are saying, or any wish to enter into dialogue with them. Further he refuses to acknowledge that the inferiority of women in the Church is an issue of justice. He made this point clearly to some American bishops in September, 1983, when they were on their *ad limina* visit to Rome.[37] His words read strangely to Christian ears. He invites the bishops to refrain from compassion with one group of people, namely women, who try to point out the injustice of their position in the Church. This lack

121

of compassion, he tells the bishops, should characterize their leadership.

Nevertheless, some bishops and some Conferences of Bishops have begun to demonstrate some of this compassion. Some structures for dialogue have been set up by both the American and Canadian bishops, giving evidence of a need to enter into conversation with women as individuals. Some individual bishops in pastoral letters acknowledge the injustice and sinful infidelity of present Church structures with regard to women. Archbishop Hayes of Halifax wrote: "The Church that is experienced today is one that comes out of a male dominated tradition. It is a Church that has been male-organized, male-led, male-taught, and male-celebrated. . . We relegate our teaching and our preaching to males and experience too much of our belief from the head and not enough from the heart. We formulate and organize a liturgy that is led by a man who has rarely, if ever, laid a table or fed a family from his own efforts and so we celebrate a liturgy in which the reality of meal is unrecognizable."[38]

Archbishop Hunthausen, in his pastoral letter on women in 1980 wrote: "We cannot expect women to accept a role that limits their growth, opportunity, freedom, dignity and particularly, their rights. . . Change is mandated. In this regard we cannot afford not to change." In response to their archbishop's letter, the priests of eight parishes published a letter which concluded with the following prayer: "Loving God, we cannot change the past, or erase the memories of oppression and insensitivity. But we do repent and beg forgiveness. Prod us when we are tempted to sin again. And we prayerfully ask all women with whom and to whom we minister to be their brothers' keepers, so that together we can create the future. Amen."[39]

And finally, at the Synod in 1983, the Canadian bishops added to their fine history of statements in support of women's journey towards full inclusion in the Church. The bishops spoke: "As for us, let us recognize the ravages of sexism and our own male appropriation of Church institutions and numerous aspects of the Christian life. Need I mention the example of the masculine language of our official—and even liturgical—texts?" In another part of the statement, the Canadian bishops showed that they are willing to move beyond the "special nature" and limited equality of women in the Church. It makes a good and hopeful closing for our chapter on Church teaching: "A new humanity is being realized in Jesus Christ in which internal conflicts of racial, social and sexual origin are abolished; a new humanity responsible for bringing about its own historical and cultural existence. In this humanity man and woman come into being and recognize each other on a basis of equality of origin and destiny, and equality in mission and involvement."[40]

Chapter 8

Woman-Church Teaches

In the very brief examination of Church teaching with regard to women, it was noticed that, when the Church speaks officially, one of the constants is that while women are addressed, they are spoken to; they have not been included as partners in a dialogue. At another level, however, the voice of women is heard in our lands. It is a voice coming from below (in hierarchical terms), but in terms of the new vision from which these women speak, it is a voice coming from the center of humanity and from the center of the Church. In recent years, women have become increasingly aware that though they may have been written out of the scriptural and historical record of the Church's life, in today's Church they are present in great numbers and great variety, and the voice of Woman-Church is beginning to sound. Woman-Church speaks with an awareness that this is a new historical moment, and it was perhaps first articulated as such in 1975.

In that year a group of women gathered in Detroit, and one of their number addressed them as follows: "We are not the whole Church nor do we claim to speak for the whole Church. Some may even dispute our right to meet as a Church at all, for we have not been called together by any official or hierarchy. We would have welcomed such an invitation but none has been forthcoming. Therefore, we speak our part of the dialogue publicly, unofficially, but nonetheless as Church."[1]

Since that time in both Canada and the United States, a dialogue has been begun between the Church and Woman-Church, and the consciousness of being Church women and Woman-Church has grown in the lives and hearts of many women.[2] These are the women who speak from the third grouping of the three enumerated in the first chapter—women who, while acknowledging the historical and present marginalization of women in the Church, nevertheless claim the Church as their home. These are the women who initiated a dialogue before a dialogue was initiated. These are the women who try to live in "anticipatory obedience" to a renewed vision of Church, a vision of which we have seen some glimpses in the lives of Prisca, Phoebe, Martha, Catherine, Mary Ward, and the other foremothers of the preceding chapters. These are women who love the Church and are committed to make the work of the Church their own. But it is a Church in which women are not included as equal partners. It is, indeed, an odd position to find oneself in, to be a member of a Church where one is not officially an equal partner, but to find a consciousness of equal partnership growing in one's heart and to discover a growing empowerment from this consciousness. Woman-Church, while remaining loyal members of the Church, are also responding to the "higher obedience" which beckoned our foremothers to become makers of the Church of the future.

This chapter will look at just a few of the insights arising from Woman-Church. Chapter 9 will attempt to examine the impact of these issues at the level of the local Church. Here, however, the first point to be made is that Woman-Church demands to be taken seriously. The question of the place of women in the Church is a central issue. It is not just one among a number of issues that should eventually claim some portion of the time of Church officials. Women are convinced that the distortion of the image of humanity evident in the historical and ecclesiastical oppression of women is at the basis of all other forms of oppression. The place of its women members is a central concern of the Church. It is not a woman's problem or a woman's issue. It is a human problem and an ecclesial one.

Women feel encouraged to call the Church to a new kind of fidelity to its original mandate, the mandate articulated in the life and deeds of Jesus and the unforgettable words of Paul. It is a vision of a new community of coequal disciples. Since it is a vision of discipleship, women intend to live as disciples and to model their words, actions, and lives on the vision of the gospel as faithfully as possible. Like all disciples, women too are called to hear the Word of God and to do it faithfully. But since it is a vision of **coequal** discipleship, women are committed to live in anticipatory obedience to this vision, to find ways to act out their equality of discipleship in Jesus Christ and their equality of membership in the Church of Jesus Christ.

What is characteristic of and fundamental to all forms of Woman-Church is the denunciation of all forms of patriarchy, and its sometimes more benign ecclesiastical expression in the many forms of paternalism.[3] A system of social and ecclesiastical structuring which is based on the supposed inferiority of any group characterized by race, sex, or any other qualifier is, from the human and Christian perspective, an unjust, dehumanizing, and destructive system. Any ecclesiastical or Christian structure which affirms anything less than the full humanity of women is recognized as sinful and is to be denounced. Historical excuses can be found for such structures and political explanations. These sinful structures are not to be explained away, however; they are to be seen for what they are—sinful—and denounced as such. All the expressions of sexism which flow from these oppressive structures are likewise to be denounced. Sexism is experienced by women in such a variety of ways today, both in and out of the Church, that the tasks seem enormous. And, as many women have discovered, once one becomes sensitive to the dimensions of the problem, one is often reduced to something akin to impotent rage. The achievement of the full humanity of all apparently is not on the agenda of any other world institution either. It is up to the Christian Churches to take a stand for persons and for all the ways in which the dignity of persons is enhanced. As we have seen, this stance has characterized much of twentieth-century Church teaching. The further point being made by Woman-Church is that only women can define the dimensions of their own humanity, and this can only be done in the context of Christian dialogue within the Church.

The use of the word *denunciation* may seem excessive. It would not be considered excessive when describing the condemnation of any other obvious form of sinfulness in the Church or the world in general. It does not mean that women are marching through the Church with ringing denunciations constantly on their lips, but it does outline clearly the parameters of the discussion. What is at stake is the humanity of women, and one is entitled to some fervor when one discovers that the ways of being human for women in the Church are at present seriously circumscribed.

As in the past, women today are discovering in the tradition of Christianity powerful confirmation of the rightfulness of their vision. Feminist theologians are contributing a marvellous new mosaic of richness to the Christian life. The work of these theologians is as varied as the individuals engaged in it. Feminist theology now has a history; one can trace its development over the past few decades, and there are no signs that the richness is disappearing.[4] In fact, quite the contrary. The doing of theology by women arises from a new form of consciousness that they are not just recipients of a message preached by others, but that they too have a word to add, and a word that has not been heard before. As has been mentioned, these words are not yet "officially" heard in the Churches, but the audience is growing from below.

One of the claims of traditional theology was that it had structures by which the "pure truth" could be presented to us. We asked questions such as: "What does the Church teach on . . . ?" and we expected clear and concise answers. The interpretation, life, or sex, of the teacher was presumed to have no influence on the truth of the answer. The formal and rational processes of Thomistic theology served but to enhance this presumption on the "neutral" theologian passing on the "pure truth" of Christianity.

Feminists point out, however, that all traditional theology was the result of male reflection on male experience, communicated in textbooks written by males and intended only for males. The official teaching of the Church followed the same process. It is difficult for many people to hear the message that maleness is not a neutral factor, perhaps because the notion of rationality and maleness have been linked so consistently throughout our history. This lack of neutrality is obvious, and abundantly so, especially to those who have been excluded from the process. Traditional theology has been laden with vested interests and has served to support the spiritual life and religious experience and ecclesiastical control of the male members of the Church. This is not to deny the contributions of this theology to our history, but simply to point to the fact that a theology done by half the membership of the Church is not a theology which can possibly be faithful to the whole Christian tradition.

Women come to theology without any claim to neutrality. On the contrary women doing theology are confessedly committed to working for a new and inclusive experience of Church. Women doing theology are attempting to articulate ever more clearly the voice of Woman-Church so that women's share in the dialogue will be faithful and truthful. Women theolgians are not intent on doing theology just for women. Their voice, their hope, their concern is for a new way of being Church. The theology of Woman-Church is being done always in view of the dialogue which will lead us all to this new experience and expression of Church which will be more faithful, women believe, to the call of the gospel.

Traditional theology is based on the sources of Scripture and tradition. To these sources women add the experience of women. No matter how rich and complete traditional theology has been, it has never been able to speak from consciousness of a woman's experience of God. It is this dimension which women bring to theology. Women start from the consciousness that the image of God is fully realized in the being of women. This was basic to traditional theology. It is the first time in the history of the Church that women have claimed this principle for themselves. Women are Godlike. At times in our past it was forbidden to women to image themselves as Godlike persons. Even today the Church often seems ambivalent on this subject. Not so Woman-Church! The signature of God is written into the being of women, and through baptism their lives are fully inserted into the life, death, and resurrection of Jesus Christ. It is the full claiming of these two realities by women which provide the basis for a new theology of women, for women, and by women for the Church.

In view of all that has been said already in these pages it is easy to see that this is a new journey for women and a new journey for the whole Church. This work has not been done before; it has not been attempted before; it was never even envisaged before. In the past women were told in what ways they could or could not image God and be "in Christ." Now the hearts and lives of women are bringing an entirely new range of meaning to theology. And to this can be added the deaths of women. Women have not been strangers to martyrdom, but the killing of Christian women today—often by Christian rulers—adds a new depth of meaning to the "experience" that women bring to theology.

As women begin to speak from their experience of God, their experience of Christ, their experience of Church, and their experience of sharing with other sister and brother Christians, the newness and difficulty of this task becomes more apparent. It is not in any sense a discovery of the fidelity of women compared with the infidelity of men. Women Christians, as all Christians, know themselves to be saved sinners. In their lives, however, the dimensions of sin and the dimensions of salvation take on new aspects. The recommended vices and virtues of women have been frequent matter for traditional Christian writing, and women discover that much of this teaching has been internalized and has become part of their lives. Women discover that they have often been the kind of people they have been told to be. And they discover too that the assumption of these recommended virtues is an **infidelity** to the call of Jesus Christ. Women have internalized a range of possibilities for themselves as Christians which is often dehumanizing, but often too, strangely comfortable. Reading the Gospels with new eyes brings new challenges to women. The message of the gospel calls for radical commitment, not comfortable conformity. Women are beginning to realize the extent to which silence, demureness, submission, and all the other "feminine" virtues have become a part of their psyches. The challenge of discipleship is to hear the Word of God and do it—in all its dimensions, not in a few select instances or in a few particularly appropriate virtues. The mothering virtues do not sum up the Christian mystery for anyone.

Women discover too, as they do theology from their experience, that the male definition of sin has burned deep into their beings. Women feel in a state of un-ease or dis-ease with their bodies—those same womanly bodies which have been portrayed by centuries of Christianity as the enemy. Women have had to rediscover the graced condition of being a woman in a woman's body. Here too the image of God shines forth, as a forgotten part of our tradition tells us. "And God saw that it was very good."[5] For so many Christian teachers in the past (Augustine and Aquinas spring immediately to mind) the woman's body was an object whose main function was to be available for her husband's needs

130

and for procreation. The wishes, desires, and feelings of women, how women felt about this objectification of their bodies and persons did not enter the discussion. Even the supposedly humorous advice given to English war brides in a new world amply illustrates this—"lie on your back and think of England."

Centuries of such teaching has not been without its effect on women, and the task of reclaiming our bodies as the place of meeting God has been one of great difficulty. The oft-quoted sermon of Pope Pius XII to newly married couples sums up the substance of Church teaching to women about pregnancy. It is seen as a curse, a penalty for disobedience. "To the woman, God has reserved the labor of childbirth, the pains of breast-feeding and of the early upbringing of children. . . ."[6] This teaching affected even the medical profession where for centuries the pain of childbirth was interpreted as God's will for women and efforts to relieve such pain were often interpreted as tampering with God's will. Menstruation has been surrounded with even more taboos than pregnancy. It still lurks suspiciously close to the surface in many debates about the appropriateness of women in the sanctuary. All the female characteristics of womanhood were surrounded with a vaguely sinful aura. Images of holy women, images especially of Mary the Mother of Jesus were neutralized. No evidence of womanly characteristics remained. Many a teaching on modesty left women with a sense of the shamefulness of their bodies. It would indeed be remarkable if all this negative reinforcement of our inferior status had not influenced our sense of ourselves.

The dualism inherent in much of Christian teaching left women with a sense that they were, indeed, far from God. God was defined as spirit, woman as body. A sense of godlikeness would have been extremely difficult to develop in that context. Besides, the virtues of women were prescribed virtues. The spiritual direction of women often pointed them away from their own feelings toward a set of virtues that were alien to them. As a result, their experience became second-hand, alienated experience. The result often was that women became numb. A great deal of writing exists on women and "insanity" through history. What was counted as insanity can often be seen now as a revolt against imposed standards of behavior. Women who did not fit the prescribed mold were unfit for society. They deserved to be locked away or burnt at the stake. Freudian analysis affirmed for women that if they did not fit the prescribed formula, if they were not the "formula female," then they were obviously sick.

In the life of St. Teresa of Avila it is recorded that the major moment of conversion in her life was the conversion from a **self divided** to a **self united.** Women today experience the same conversion. But it is a never-ending task. Even in our popular wisdom the mixed messages given to women are apparent. A partial list of mixed messages would include the following:

- inferior under the law, but really controlling everything through cunning; the power behind the throne
- queen of the home, but without any real authority
- preserver of the morals of the next generation, but herself of questionable moral worth
- the weaker sex, but devastatingly dangerous when not properly supervised
- demonic yet angelic; either Eve or Mary; in the gutter or on the pedestal
- expected to be always clean of tongue, but never allowed to speak in Church
- of little intellect, but of great cunning
- lover of men, but often their destroyer or castrator
- victim of violence, but the cause of this same violence—"asking for it"
- burnt as witches, but canonized after death
- mothers of children who belong to others and bear others' names
- givers of birth, but not recognized as creative
- helpmate to the male, but his greatest threat
- holier than men, but excluded from holy places
- baptized into Christ, but not a sign of his presence
- called to be both virgin and mother
- and so on. The list is capable of almost infinite expansion.

One of the enormous benefits of the women's movement in society, and especially in the Churches, is that an opportunity is provided for women to discover these internalized divisions in the company and with the support of other women. Of even greater consequence, together women are able to rediscover the power of being women, the gracefulness of being a God-imager in a woman's body, the creativity of birth-giving. It is this latter power which is becoming a key symbol for many women. The rage of many early feminists against unjustly structured marriages has often been interpreted as the "normal" feminist approach to birth and motherhood. To a woman the difference between being a baby-machine and choosing motherhood is the difference between hell and heaven. Even within the strict realm of Roman Catholic marriage theology, a distinction is now made between the choice to marry and the choice to parent.

With minds and spirits sensitized by centuries of injustice and oppression, women bring to the exploration of their experience as humans and as Christians a new dynamism which is in the process of revitalizing theology. Although this theology is marginal in the Church as a whole, in the lives of women it has become a liberating power which assures the Church of new life, new riches, and a new and different future.

Obviously, the exploration of all the dimensions of women's experience has enormous consequence for the prayer life of the Church and for the individual and collective prayer life of women. The language of prayer will be further discussed in the next chapter. It is sufficient here to point out the difficulties of prayer life for women, given the message about themselves communicated by the Church. How do women pray at a male-led liturgy, worship a God addressed only in male language, enter into public prayer which can be led and articulated only by ordained males, expressing the experiences and reflection of these males? How have women prayed when in their prayer they have been invited to pray as "brothers" for the maturity of "sons" of God? How have women experienced the Christian mystery when it is expressed always in terms of "becoming a son" or growing into the "fullness of sonship"? How have women listened to the Word of God when the invitation to listen has always begun with the words "my brothers"? How have women prayed when they have been instructed to be silent in the churches? How have women experienced their baptism when they have been told that even as baptized they do not represent Christ?

"If the image of God is found in woman as well as in man, both the male and female metaphors will have to be used to speak of God."[7] If God is to be imaged in both male and female terms, then the nuptial language which always uses God as bridegroom cannot be the normative language of our faith. In a patriarchal

133

structure, this kind of language made some kind of sense. In a community of coequal disciples, the God-language will have to be more faithful to the language of Jesus. It is to this that we now turn.

If God is to be seen as a patriarchal father, then a religion of obedience is the obvious response. Attitudes of fear, awe, and reverence predominate among the worshippers. The dispensing of judgment, spectacular displays of power, wrathful displays of vengeance when wronged, absolute commands, and infinite knowledge characterize the God worshipped. If God is this kind of patriarchal father, then the word and experience of liberation are a mockery. Life is static. It is to be accepted; one has to be resigned to one's lot, an attitude of unquestioning obedience is the most lauded virtue. There is no doubt that some of these elements have characterized our attitudes towards God. As Dorothy Solle has said so well, "Obedience is no longer a theologically innocent word after the Holocaust."[8] Obedient Christians, brought up in a Catholic culture of obedience, implemented the Holocaust. The common excuse offered for participation in the horror was "we were only obeying orders." Obviously there is a Christian obedience that bears no relationship whatever to these attitudes, but which of us can easily affirm that we practice the one and not the other?

We must ask ourselves if this is the God of Jesus Christ? Does obedience to a Father-God in an authoritarian Church constitute the heart of the Christian message? For members on the levels where nothing but obedience is expected—and women have always and essentially been there—is the only norm for the Christian life a norm of self-denial? Are self-realization and resistance the main sins or the main virtues?

Scripture scholars have pointed out that the main characteristic of the God of the Hebrews was election. God chose, elected a people to covenant with. As Father, God is not spoken of in terms of generation, but in terms of election, of liberation, of covenant. God is Father of a new creation, of a new covenant. In the New Testament, the word *Father* is found on the lips of Jesus 170 times as a form of address for God.[9] It was apparently the best biblical word to characterize the novelty of the God of Jesus. But it is always an invocation, a form of address, and never a substantive statement. On the lips of Jesus and in his parables, this Father is never a patriarchal father. The Prodigal Son, or Prodigal Father, in Luke's parable should illustrate this abundantly. The God imaged by Jesus and addressed as *Father* is a God who cannot control his loving impulses. He throws parties for repentant sinners. He restores wandering children to the household. His care reaches out to the sinful and to those religiously excluded.

The particular sign of this extraordinary new relationship with God in the language of Jesus is the word *Abba*. Jesus was not speaking of the God of philosophy. He was not making metaphysical statements. He was not stating that God is anything. Jesus uses *Abba* as a **metaphor** for a relationship. It is a metaphor for a moment of recognition, of **mutual** recognition. On the lips of Jesus, God as Abba is the metaphor for a new kind of religious existence. We are called to new life, not like our former life of infantile dependency, but to a new life of mutuality. Human beings can be comfortable and feel graced in the presence of such a God. For a God such as this, the attributes of justice, love, compassion, and reconciliation are more important than the attributes of infinite power and infinite knowledge. Such a God calls us as partners in this relationship to Godlike works—to love tenderly and to act justly.

New metaphors are needed to speak of such a God. The word *father*, as we have come to understand it in a patriarchal sense, may inhibit our mutual relationship with this God rather than facilitate it. Perhaps speaking of God as *Mother* also will restore to our consciousness and to our imagination some of the meaning conveyed by Jesus in his favorite word for God—*Abba.*

Another far from easy task presents itself here to the women and men of today's Church. A new power of prayer is being found when women gather to pray in a conscious effort to be faithful to their full humanity. Women discover that they have been observers at liturgical prayer. The sense of participation that comes with creating new symbols and new prayer forms breaks open the divine-human relationship in myriad ways. When voices that have been silent begin to speak of God, when the silence of centuries is broken, Women-Church begins to take shape. Hearing each other speak and pray empowers women to probe new depths of understanding, to claim new historical powers, to accept unheard of responsibility for the coming of the kingdom. Breaking the silence of centuries awakens women to the other unheard voices,

135

and with this awakening, a new sense of solidarity with all the silent suffering of the world is realized. Because women have known and experienced exclusion in prayer, they now consciously try to practice inclusion. The word *neighbor* receives a new definition. It no longer means those who are near us, those like us, those around us, those with whom we are comfortable, but the word is changed radically to include all the "others," those excluded, those whose words and stories have not been heard.

The ancient symbols of our faith come to life anew when they are allowed to be recreated from the experience of women. We have seen that Archbishop Hayes indicated something of this nature when he spoke of liturgies celebrated by males who had never prepared a meal for a family. Women know about meals. In their hands, a liturgical celebration of sharing bread reveals levels of meaning undreamt of in the formalized ritual of the Sunday celebration. So many dimensions of these realities have faded from our consciousness. Women, faced with the task of creating a language of prayer, can bring to the Church new richness of liturgical experience. The only question that remains is the age-old one—will this richness be recognized and welcomed as integral to the ancient prayer of the Church?

In this chapter we have raised a few of the issues that are surfacing in Woman-Church as a result of a newly awakened consciousness of Christian women. These are the women who, despite their realization of oppressive structures and especially those operative within Roman Catholicism, nevertheless determine to remain within the Church. And their reason for remaining is simple. The Church is women's Church. Within the Christian tradition there is also to be found a great message and experience of liberation. Many women have experienced this liberating gift— if only in glimpses and moments—but sufficiently to know the freeing power of the gospel of Jesus Christ, and to know that within the *ecclesia* this gospel can still be preached.

In order for this new Church, which will be a community of coequal disciples, to come about, centuries of dialogue will be necessary. What is essential is that it be begun.

We close this chapter with statements of two persons who were presented before the world as being in opposition to one another on the subject of the role of women in the Church—Pope

John Paul II and Sister Theresa Ann Kane. Sister Kane spoke to the Pope in Washington as follows:

> I call upon you to listen with compassion and to hear the call of women, who comprise half of humankind. As women we have heard the powerful messages of our Church addressing the dignity and reverence for all persons. As women we have pondered upon these words. Our contemplation leads us to state that the Church in its struggle to be faithful to its call for reverence and dignity for all persons must respond by providing the possibility of women as persons being included in all ministries of our church.[10]

During the same visit to the United States, Pope John Paul, speaking in Chicago said:

> Love is the power that gives rise to dialogue, in which we listen to each other and learn from each other. Love gives rise, above all, to the dialogue of prayer in which we listen to God's Word, which is alive in the Holy Bible and alive in the life of the Church.
>
> Let love, then, build the bridges across our differences and, at times, our contrasting positions. Let love for each other and love for the truth be the answer to polarization when factions are formed because of differing views in matters that are related to faith or to priorities for action.[11]

Woman-Church brings to the dialogue these same convictions and these same hopes. And if all parties are led by the same Spirit, inspired by the same hope and fired by the same love, then a dialogue once begun can only lead to a new understanding and a new realization of the word of Jesus: "May they all be one."

Chapter 9

Pray, My Sisters and Brothers

During the past twenty years, women have begun to do theology in significance and numbers unparalleled in any other time
in Christian history.[1] This is fact of recent history, and both the
numbers and significance give promise only of continued growth.
At the same time, there is testimony on all sides that women are
leaving the Church in unparalleled numbers and that the significance of this has not yet been grasped fully by the Church.[2]

In many ways, the exodus of women represents a new ingredient in the experience of the Church. Many of the women
see themselves as **seceding,** not drifting away, but consciously
feeling the need to separate themselves from an oppressive structure, one which has become all the more oppressive because its
very nature promises liberation and reconciliation to all. The new
willingness of the Church today to enter into dialogue and to celebrate gestures of reconciliation with persons and groups for-
merly far from the Church's ken—people from all creeds, all
political persuasions, all walks of life—is a source of joy to all. But
one group, fully constituting half of the membership of the
Church, is excluded from such dialogue. Surely this is a cause for
repentance, forgiveness, and new efforts.

This final chapter will touch on some of the areas which affect the life of the local Church in a particular way. If women have
walked away there, it is usually without fanfare. If there are no
ecclesiastical structures of dialogue on a large scale in the Church,

then even more obviously, lacking leadership and incentive, there are none at the local level. Besides, the very busy-ness of most parishes and their leaders tend to reprioritize the tasks of the Christian community. What is most urgent at the moment receives attention and tends to drain all the energies. This is understandable, and, in our broken world, it is good to know that there are places where a few cries, at least, can be heard. This is not, however, a Church that is preparing for the future. It is merely exhausting all its resources—more and more limited in terms of personnel—on the present. There is no time to stand back to get a larger view. There is no time to evaluate what is being done or left undone. There is no time to meditate on the challenges of the gospel for today's world. There is no time to hope. The model of a local Church is that of hospital and not dynamic community. Once the local Church begins to see itself and actually reorganizes itself as local community, the underlying pathology comes to light. This has happened in many instances with the incorporation of the Rite of Christian Initiation of Adults into parish life.[3]

Many women are walking away from local parishes, and it is often the women who have tried to become most involved in ministry to the community, or who desire and feel called to this involvement. These are the women who have experienced rejection and who are most alienated. It is in the local parish that most women live and celebrate their faith, and for many women this living and this celebrating are becoming more and more problematic. In many instances, these women have never heard of feminist analysis; if confronted with the expression "Woman-Church," they might not recognize its import. But in their lives they have run up against the exclusion of women. Their tragedy is that they have not experienced any support system. They walk away alone, and not long after them will walk their daughters and younger sisters. Alienation, of its very nature, does not seek solutions. These are sought only where there is a supportive community. It is such a support group who, as mentioned in the first chapter of this volume, announced to the local Churches which they represent throughout Canada that they are considering "withholding their dollars from collection plates." This is not an effort to destroy the finances of the Church. It is a call to dialogue.

A choice among issues has to be made for discussion in our final chapter. It is an arbitrary choice, but the four issues chosen will be significant to every woman in every parish in the Christian world. They are the stuff of our daily life—language, ministry, sexual violence, and marriage. Before dealing with these issues it will be appropriate to reproduce here the plan of action of one group of priests in the Archdiocese of Seattle. They outlined for themselves ten commitments growing from their realization of the need to struggle in the Church for justice for women.[4]

1. *During the period of waiting for official translations we will try to use inclusive language in preaching, teaching and every form of written discourse. As priests, we invite our various publics to help us to be creative in our language as we foster a faith founded on a Word become flesh.*
2. *Recognizing that theologically no one term captures the reality of God, we will try to speak of our common God in terms that free the Spirit. God is Father, but also Mother, Creator, Merciful, Loving, Challenging. . . . We will search for inclusive ways to speak to and about God as we pray publicly on behalf of a community of both men and women.*
3. *We will continue to try to assure women of equal opportunities for ministry within the Church and the remuneration these ministries deserve, and to open to women positions previously held only by men, e.g., chaplaincies in hopsitals and jails, and various other parish ministries.*
4. *We will seek to establish equal representation of women on councils, commissions, boards and task-forces on every level of parish and archdiocesan concern.*
5. *We will continue to address the question of women in the Church, and to speak openly about injustices of the past and dreams for the future.*
6. *We will invite women to speak within Church services, letting the gifts of women break open the Word of God to enrich us not only on women's issues but on the entire spectrum of our mutual pastoral concerns.*
7. *We will continue our effort to avoid male dominance in liturgical settings, fostering the use of women as trained cantors, ushers, lectors, greeters, Eucharistic ministers, servers, and by using care concerning the appropriateness of concelebrations, and the visibility of clergy when concelebrations do occur.*

8. *We will continue to encourage women to: bring Eucharist to sick and shut-in parishioners, lead Eucharistic services when no priest is available, act as counselors, retreat directors, spiritual directors, teachers of theology.*
9. *We will search for ways to include women within the celebration of the Sacrament of the Sick, and communal celebrations of the Sacrament of Reconciliation, affirming the gifts of healing that are theirs.*
10. *We will struggle for equality for women in whatever ways we can.*

In the preceding chapter and often throughout this small volume the question of language in the Church has been referred to. In many ways, this is one of the foundational questions. If we are often assured that the "women in my parish are happy and do not want any changes," it is more than likely that (1) the parish leaders are not aware of the alienated members of the parish, or that (2) the members of the parish, particularly the women, have been anaesthetized by the overwhelming maleness of the public worship of the Catholic Church into a position of numbness and insensitivity. This is precisely the effect of exclusive language in liturgy. Its effects are exactly as indicated by the word *exclusive*. In order to be included, women have to perform continual mental gymnastics, and this during every prayer, every reading, every creed, every prayer of consecration, and often even during every prayer of reconciliation. So many liturgies of reconciliation in parishes end by inviting all to live in harmony as "brothers." No wonder, then, that women may never have noticed that they are not included, or if they have noticed, they have tired of the endless effort at self-inclusion.

Other women continue a solo effort of retranslating as they go along, contributing a slightly disruptive element to the devotions of their immediate neighbors as they sing about the "Faith of our **Mothers**" and of how "God made **us** in His own image, gave **us** power to think and choose, made **us** lords of all creation, everything is **ours** to use."

The fundamental question of language, however, has not been faced by the Churches. Theorists tell us that the language of a people indicates what is important to them. "The more important the item, the more varied the language."[5] The example usually given by way of illustration is the usage in Eskimo culture of

142

eighteen different words for *snow*. For most of us, one word is more than enough. Another example is the numerous annual additions to the automobile vocabulary of the average American. Our liturgical language follows the same linguistic rules; it finds words for what is important. And women are almost totally excluded from this language. One might say that in **principle** they are totally excluded. In the language of the Church, women do not exist. The history of women in the Church is reenacted every time a liturgy is celebrated, every time a public prayer in exclusive language is uttered. In the language of the Church, God saves **men;** Jesus came "for us **men** and for our salvation;" the blood of the "new and everlasting covenant" was shed for all **men**—and this, in most places, in spite of recent changes; the readings at liturgies are addressed to the "brothers," and the use of words like *disciple* and *apostle*, so liberally sprinkled throughout our liturgical celebrations, are intended to be interpreted as pointing only to males. In addition, the Eucharistic prayers emphasize the prayers for the clergy—the second Eucharistic prayer does not even mention living lay members of the Church, but prays simply for the living clergy and the dead "brothers and sisters." Exclusive language in the hymn selections in the average liturgy are usually too numerous for even the most avid feminist to notice.

What is the result of this language barrage? Language is not neutral. It not only expresses what we believe, it shapes our thoughts and beliefs. What is expressed in our liturgical language is that the liturgy is mostly for men. What is shaped by our liturgical language is the conviction that this is the way our liturgy is going to stay. This fact is all the more devastating when we consider the importance of the Mass in the lives of Catholics. It is the high point of our communal expression of our relationship with God and the high point in the expression of the totality of the Christian mystery. At the most important moment in the life of the local Church, women are excluded, they are nonpersons. If the Eucharist is the "looking-glass" of the Christian life, then women find there no reflection at all.

Another result of exclusive language, besides the erasure of women from the communal consciousness during the Eucharistic celebration, is that women are not challenged by the Word of God. The presence of women at liturgy—though usually they are in the majority—is peripheral. They are observers. The language of prayer and Scripture does not hit home. Women, when addressed as brothers, are thereby rendered almost incapable of really hearing the Word of God. It does not penetrate to the heart. The practice of Jesus, as has been seen, was different. His words were addressed specifically to the women and the men. On the face of it, what could be the reason for resisting the use of inclusive language? Women are not asking for a few centuries of female sexist language. They are asking for inclusive language. A simple use of the first person plural or the pronoun "them" would solve most of the problem. But the resistance to such simple solutions is enormous. The issue at stake is truly of enormous consequence—a change in language represents a journey from an exclusive, male-dominated concept of Church organized on patriarchal lines to an inclusive community-conscious vision of Church, characterized by the active reaching out to all persons.

Not only is the ongoing use of sexist language continuing to deform the spiritual consciousness of both the women and the men who come to celebrate the Eucharist, but the continued unwillingness of the Church at both universal and local levels to change sends a clear message about what is considered important in the Church. As we have said, we find language for what is important to us.

Centuries of Christian anthropoligical writing point to the intellect and the use of language in particular as the most characteristic human attribute. Language releases the spirit, as the moving story of Helen Keller illustrates so well. The demands of our modern life are forcing us to change our language in many areas, and to recognize the limited range of meaning imposed on some very common words. Two of the most common must surely be *father* and *mother*. *Fathering* a child has traditionally come to mean giving life to a child; *mothering* a child means caring for the child. In this sense, *mothering* is often used with negative overtones of spoiling the child. This is common usage, although the dictionary definitions give an altogether different range of meaning. Our culture is discovering a larger set of meaning for both words as more and more households become single-parent establishments. What is most surprising is that the popular usage of the words has taken all the life-giving and creative content from mothering, where it obviously belongs, and "mothering" becomes a not very noble pursuit. The word *father* has been endowed with all the meaning which even biologically is impossible, but so reminiscent of our friend Thomas Aquinas. This usage constitutes something of a reversal myth similar to the story of Adam and Eve, where the normal processes of a mother giving birth are reversed and the man gives birth to the woman. No wonder this has become Christianity's favorite myth for the founding of the race!

Such a brief example illustrates the wonderful workings of our language. Language is not neutral; in fact, language tells us what to think and who we are to be. Women need to continue the search for new ways to express their identity, creating, if necessary, a new language to express their newly discovered being and newly found gracefulness in God's presence. And let the male-led Church follow the example of their brothers in Seattle whose commitments were enumerated at the beginning of this chapter. In the process, nothing will be lost except injustice and the anonymity of half the human race and half the Christian Church. What will be gained will be a community of disciples celebrating the discipleship of equals.

The most valuable resource of the Church is its people. The process of caring for these people, of encouraging them, of challenging them, of healing them, of proclaiming the Word of God with them, and of celebrating with them has been called by generations of Christians the practice of ministry. Ministry became ordered in the early church as a multi-faceted response to the growing needs of the rapidly expanding Christian community. The basic process was crystal clear in its simplicity. The Spirit of God, alive in the community, endowed persons with different gifts. Growing communities in different cultures and different geographic locations experienced a variety of needs. The Spirit-given gifts were linked with the needs. And so new communities experienced ministry.

One might ask why such a simple solution does not work today. The needs are obvious. The same Spirit is still present and active in the community—why not then the same multifaceted ministry? We saw something of the process of the exclusion of women from ministry in earlier chapters. Ministry, instead of being a mutual sharing of gifts of the Spirit, came to be organized along patriarchal lines, and this meant it was reorganized on the principle of power. One had to have power to minister; gifts were no longer sufficient. Along the same patriarchal lines, all manner of people were excluded from the exercise of power, and primary among the powerless, generically so, were the women. It is this fact which makes the question of ministry in the Roman Catholic Church such a thorny issue. The very word *ministry* was confined for centuries to the ordained clergy. What was asked of other Christians was service. And since patriarchy further decreed that in families, the fathers should work "in the world," most of the service in the Church was done—and still continues to be done—by women.

A strange thing happened, though, on the way to the church basement. Women began to read the Scriptures, and were newly sensitized to the power and presence of the Spirit in their lives. And women came to name the work they were doing *ministry*. And those who were healed, catechized, fed, treated justly, called to peace, and reconciled, experienced ministry from women. Likewise, those who hear women proclaim the Word of God at liturgy, those who receive Eucharist from the hands of women, those who are led in liturgical song by women, those who are counseled by women, those who are helped to pray by women— all of these experience ministry. And groups of women who have never been ministered to before are now experiencing ministry from their sisters—battered wives; lesbian women; divorced, separated, and remarried women; prostitutes, and other street women.

One would expect that the next paragraph might add that the Church rejoices greatly at this new and great diversity of talent. And in one sense it does. But the most usual experience of the women ministers is that their ministry causes some anxiety in the Churches. It is hedged around with so many **caveats** lest women appear too active, too visible, too priestly, too powerful. Women are advised to play a "low key" role since "there are some who do not like women ministers." Where affirmation is called for, where support is expected, women often find instead that the opposing elements are the ones reinforced by the clergy.

In a sometimes comic way, the issue of ministry seems to revolve around two extremes—the issue of the ordination of women and the issue of altar girls. Both issues have been divisive in many communities, and the question of the ordination of women remains the single most explosive issue in the Roman Catholic Church. After years of attempting to explain away altar girls, and after sometimes polarizing local communities on this issue, most Church leaders have now backed off and treat the presence of altar girls with a kind of benign neglect. The most oft-repeated responses to requests for approval of altar girls, however, throw much light on the issues of ministry in a larger sense. It is argued that at the "altar-boy age" girls are generally more reliable, more gifted, and simply more competent than boys. If girls, therefore, are allowed to minister at the altar they will soon outshine and outnumber the boys. Better then to go with the less talented and less reliable boys in order to keep them "interested." And many fathers and mothers rejoice greatly because, as they so rightly say, "This is the only way I can get him to church." A second form of argumentation went from the presence of boys in church and on the altar to seeing the time spent as altar boy as minor seminary training—it prepared boys to be future priests. It was a junior form of the "old boys network."

And what of girls? What of this talent and commitment? Did anyone care if they stayed or left? Apparently not, for no alternate ministry was, to my knowledge, ever offered to them. The presence of girls in the church and on the alter is not as vital to the Church as the presence of boys. The commitment of girls is not real commitment. The ministry of girls is not real ministry. The exodus of girls is not as much a loss. The presence of the Spirit in girls is not as spiritual as the presence of the Spirit in boys.

All of these comments have been formulated by girls of "altar-boy age" who even at the age of ten do not accept the sometimes apologetic, sometimes dictatorial, explanations for the lack of welcome offered to them by the Church. Add to these comments the maturity, theological formation, ministerial experience, lifetime commitments of Spirit-filled Christian women, and the question of the exclusion of women from ministry, ordained and otherwise, in the Roman Catholic Church takes on the dimensions of a scandal. For the reasons given for the exclusion of women from ordained ministry are no more cogent and no more

Christian that the reasons offered to their daughters and younger sisters who want to be altar girls.

The whole ministry of women is not summed up in the ordination question, but there it is symbolized in a most exquisitely clear way. I hasten to add also that the question of ordination is so much more than a symbol to hundreds of Roman Catholic women who feel called to priesthood in the Church and who experience only rejection.[6] The development of the ordination debate served to alert both women and men in the Church to the true dimensions of the absence of women from the life of the Church. What was once understood as the simple inclusion of women in the present structure of ordained clergy, has now opened up the depths of division—and the horizons of possibility—within the Church. Exclusion of women raises questions about God and the imaging of God; about Christ and the discipleship of Christ; about baptism and its supposedly lesser efficacy in the lives of women than of men; about priesthood as an absolutely distinguishing characteristic of the Christian life to such a degree that there are now two classes of Christians—the ordained and the lay; about prayer and how it is led and articulated and by whom; about the public worship of the Church and about what is at the moment being celebrated by this public worship or celebrated by only half the Christian community in a language that includes only half the membership.

Such questions—and so many more—are summed up in the question of justice. This is one dimension that Pope John Paul II has specifically excluded from the discussion.[7] That in itself does not mean that ordination is not a justice issue. It so obviously fits all the other definitions of injustice and oppression contained in so many papal documents—the discrimination against a whole group by reason of their sex only.

What is glorious about the present life of the Church is that women have, in fact, accumulated for the first time in history a great store of experience in ministry. Women can now describe their ministries, can affirm each others' ministries. Women have experienced affirmation in ministry in so many situations—in prisons, church basements, classrooms, families, counseling offices, war-torn countries, barrios, hospitals, with the dying and the starving. In so many countries, Christianity depends for its continuity on the witness of faithful women. The sisters followers of women like Mary Ward and Madame d'Houet and a host of others outnumber many times over the ordained clergy. And all of this, without any doubt whatever, is in fidelity to the mandate of the Church to continue the mission of Jesus Christ.

One aspect of the oppression of women which has lacked ethical and ministerial attention in a most glaring manner has been violence against women and children, especially girl children. It is an area where women have ministered to women in non-Church situations, without very much support from either Church or state. This violence—sexual and otherwise—has been the unmentionable sin. The blame for rape, one of the most obnoxious forms of violence against women, has traditionally been assigned to the victim. Why then should any attempt be made to minister to her? A friend tells of a rape victim who ventured to Church on a Sunday morning only to be publicly blamed and summarily dismissed by the presiding priest.

The sin at the core of patriarchy is most evident in sexual violence against women. A structure of relationships which is built on the inferiority and weakness of women leads inevitably to the victimization of women. Patriarchal systems have always assured men that they have a right to violence in the pursuit of what they need, and that no home is automatically immune to this kind of violation.

This violent situation has only recently come to public attention in Canada, and the dimensions of the problem have been revealed to be far greater than anyone imagined. Fully one-quarter of all girls and women will experience some form of violence during their lifetime, usually in the privacy of their home. Women have suffered alone and have often been made to feel that they deserve this suffering. Men have been socialized not to see violence against women as an outrage. So many women and young girls who have reported such crimes to pastors, teachers, or representatives of the legal and medical professions have often been accused of fabricating lies and sent back with pious admonitions to endure further violence. Fortunately, laws have recently moved to prevent this kind of response.

The recognition of the reality of domestic violence against women and children quickly shatters the traditional image of the "good Catholic family," an image projected especially in the nineteenth and twentieth centuries. As has already been seen in some

Catholic anti-suffrage writings, the lessening of "iron discipline" was lamented.[8] It would be untrue to say that the Church supported violence against women—at least in modern times—but it would certainly be true to say that the Church supported only one family structure—the patriarchal—which had a built-in proclivity towards violence because it was based on relationships of dominance and subordination. And it would also be true to say that whenever violence was brought to the attention of the community, it was seen as occasional, deserved, and perversely enjoyed by the victims. In any event, few voices were ever raised to denounce this violence, and today are still not heard. A recent publication spoke of this unmentionable sin and quoted pastors as saying "no one ever comes to me with this problem."[9] The conclusion, then, very often is that no such problem exists. "The silence is not an indication of the absence of a problem; it is itself a loud orchestrated denial of a problem which certainly exists."[10] There is no language for speaking about this problem. The victimization of girls and women has not been important in this society.

Victims, themselves, have understandably tended to keep quiet, internalizing the situation as their own personal problem. It was not until women began to speak to other women about the violence in their homes that the true dimensions of the problem became apparent, and shelter, support, and therapy were provided. And those involved in this work believe that what they see is just the tip of the iceberg. The financial and spiritual supports of the community are slow in coming. As for the politicians, the problem of domestic violence against women and children has no more significance than a locker-room joke.

The problem has been further hidden by our habit of speaking of "normal" sexual relationships in both secular and ecclesial contexts. Sex is understood as a process in which males take the initiative, are manly and aggressive. Women, on the other hand are receptive, and "nice" women always demonstrate a certain reluctance. The myth explains that when a man forces his attentions on a woman sexually, she is always grateful and relieved. In this perspective, then, sexual violence and rape are seen as instances of things "getting a little out of hand," but otherwise normal.

But women have succeeded in showing that violence against women, even where genital activity is present, is not a sexual act, but a violent act.[11] The intent is always to overpower, to demean, to hurt, to reduce the woman to the level of an object. Any woman who has experienced rape will testify to the truth of this. The legal and medical professions are coming to recognize the truth of this position and to legislate and treat on this basis. The blatant imputation of guilt to the victim and the frequent exoneration of the rapist is no longer as easily justified legally. Nevertheless, the prosecution of a rape suspect is still a horrendous experience for any victim.

Domestic sexual violence is a little more complex both in its motivation and in its prosecution. Many men in the Roman Catholic tradition have been led to claim the prerogative of forcing their sexual needs on their wives regardless of their wishes. The confusion of male/female roles and the stereotyping of male/female characteristics cloud most situations. The main point however, is clear. When a woman—be she wife or child—is forced to submit to sex against her will by husband, or, in the case of children, by father or other relative, a violent crime has been committed and a sin against the dignity of persons has been perpetrated. This crime and this sin must be loudly denounced. Violence is not a part of "normal" sexual activity. The silence must be broken and women and child victims must be assured of the pastoral concern of the Church. The feelings of guilt, shame, uncleanness, abandonment by God, and, later, anger and possible hatred can only be healed in the context of a loving and nonjudgmental community.

The positive dimensions of human sexual relationships are badly in need of airing in our parishes. It is impossible to proclaim marriage as a celebration of the union of two persons, equal in dignity and worth before God, and at the same time to presume patriarchal marriage structures based precisely on the inequality of the partners. All possible doubt must be removed about the equal sharing of the wife in all aspects of the marriage covenant. A free partnership cannot be celebrated and lived in a dominant-subordinate situation. In the past, the Church advocated freely and openly the headship of the male, and both men and women accommodated themselves to this model, sometimes with mutual agreement, sometimes to the great hurt of both, and usually to the diminution of the woman. Today, however, the Church proclaims the equal dignity of all persons, but at the same time, as has been shown, continues to debate whether or not women are fully persons.

In the United States a pastoral letter on the personhood of women will take four years to prepare. What cannot wait any longer is the advocacy by the Church of the cause of women. And what cannot wait is the preaching and proclaiming of a new kind of marriage relationship. In this instance the preaching and proclaiming will have to be done by the participants—those who from the center of their married lives can reflect on the Christian dimensions of this experience. Only married Christian persons can fully reflect on the Christian experience of marriage with a full understanding of what this relationship entails. Only married persons can give to the Church a renewed theology of marriage. Then perhaps we shall know what Jesus meant when he said: "The kingdom of heaven is like a wedding banquet."[12]

Epilogue

We end by returning to the beginning and remembering again. And this time we remember one of the women who has been most maligned by our memories—Mary Magdalene. She is remembered as the sinner, as indeed, the prototype of Christian women sinners, and antithesis of the other Mary, the Virgin Mary. She has been the source, too, of a whole corpus of typically Catholic literature about prostitutes with hearts of gold. This is what Christianity has made of Mary Magdalene—she is a product of male fantasy, and an instrument for reminding women of their tragic flaw.

But the Mary Magdalene of the Gospel stories bears no resemblance whatever to the woman who is a creation of a patriarchal Church. In the Gospels, she is the woman who stood by Jesus throughout his life. She had been healed by Jesus, Luke tells us, and automatically it is assumed that she was healed of sin, more particularly sexual sin. The text does not necessarily imply any such thing. But for a Church tradition which grew to fear the sexuality of women as one of the greatest evils, the seven devils of the gospel text from which Magdalene was healed, could only have been interpreted as sexual sin. So Mary Magdalene was identified as the great and repentant sinner, and drew to herself all manner of other identifications from the Gospels.

In the Gospels, Mary Magdalene was always mentioned as the first person in any listing of the women around Jesus. She was obviously the leader of the group throughout the period of the public ministry, but she really came into her own in the events of Easter morning. She was the one chosen to announce the Good News to the other disciples, or as the early Church called her, the "apostle to the apostles." Mary and the other women are portrayed as the ones who remained faithful, not understanding, but persevering in their allegiance to Jesus. The male disciples are portrayed as the ones who ran way, who gave up, who returned with astonishing swiftness to business as usual.

Mary Magdalene, then, was the first Christian apostle, the first to meet and proclaim the Risen Jesus. Christian tradition and legend gives this privilege to Mary the Mother of Jesus, but there is no scriptural record of this. Mary, the Mother of Jesus, had a different mission. But Scripture does testify to the privilege accorded to one who has been, at another level, known to history as the closest friend of Jesus. While the Scriptures record the betrayal, denial, and abandonment of the male disciples, they record with equal vividness the friendship, loyalty and maturing friendship of the women disciples.

Here is a new beginning for the history of the Church, a new starting point. New models of christian discipleship are presented to women in these strong biblical women—models of friendship, human love, perseverance, fidelity, and the hard lesson of letting go when the time comes. Throughout the history examined here, we have seen other models—of apostles and preachers; dragon-slayers and martyrs; confidantes and challengers of popes and saviors of kings and nations; active missionaries and inspired teachers. Each provides us with a new vision of what is possible, a new model for the living out of the Christian mystery. Each inspires us to move forward toward the end of the twentieth century, confident that when the dragons appear, we shall overcome.

Notes

Chapter 1: In God's Own Image

1. Pope Pius XII "Allocution to Newly-Weds," par. 82 (September 10, 1941). *The Woman in the Modern World,* selected and arranged by the Monks of Solesmes, St. Paul Editions (Boston: Daughters of St. Paul 1959), 68ff.
2. Quoted in *Origins,* vol. 13, no. 19 (October 20, 1983): 335.
3. Michael McAteer of the *Toronto Star* is reporting on the conference organized by the Canadian Catholics for Womens' Ordination held in Toronto from June 29 to July 1, 1984.
4. These comments are based on reportage in Canadian newspapers over the past few years.
5. The words are taken from Andrew M. Greeley, *The Mary Myth: On the Femininity of God* (New York: Seabury Press, 1977), 106.
6. Cardinal Carter in his pastoral letter, *Do This in Memory of Me* (December 8, 1983). His words are on page 39: "The current focus for the secular revision of Church structures is the drive for the ordination. The literature upon this subject is extensive. If little of it is of much theological depth it is nonetheless important by reason of its mass and its wide appeal."
7. Pope John Paul II speaking to some American bishops on September 5, 1983.
8. What follows depends in large part on the analysis of Christian feminism by Elisabeth Schussler Fiorenza in the introductory chapters of her outstanding book *In Memory of Her,* (New York: Crossroads, 1983).
9. "The Role of Women in Evangelization" from the Pastoral Commission of the Vatican Congregation for the Evangelization of Peoples, quoted in *Origins,* vol. 5 (April 22, 1975): 703ff.
10. Closing message of Vatican II to Women, Austin Flannery, O.P. general editor, *Vatican Council II: The Conciliar and Post-Conciliar Documents* (Collegeville, Minn.: The Liturgical Press, 1975), 106.
11. See especially, Nadine Foley, "Women in Vatican Documents 1960 to the Present", in James Coriden, editor, *Sexism and Church Law* (Ramsey, N.J.: Paulist Press, 1977), 82–108.
12. The expression comes from Madonna Kolbenschlag, *Kiss Sleeping Beauty Good-Bye* (New York: Bantam Books, 1979), 11.
13. It is difficult to document the numbers of such women, but see the recent research by the Canadian Bishops' task force on women. *Report* (1983): 12ff.
14. Fiorenza, *In Memory of Her, passim.* See also, Elisabeth Schussler Fiorenza,

"Feminist Theology as a Critical Theology of Liberation," *Theological Studies,* vol. 36 (December 1975): 605–626.

15. The classic analysis of patriarchy is in Eva Figes, *Patriarchal Attitudes* (Salem, N.H.: Virago, 1970).
16. Pius XII "Allocution," *Woman in the Modern World,* par. 83.
17. See note 2 above.
18. "Pastoral Constitution on the *Church in the Modern World,*" Austin Flannery, O.P., general editor, Vatican Council II: The Conciliar and Post-Conciliar Documents (Collegeville, Minn.: The Liturgical Press, 1975), par. 2,3.
19. The starting point for all discussion about women is motherhood. See Paul VI in his address to Italian Catholic Jurists in December, 1972, in which he pinpointed the "essentially specific" aspect of "female personality" as "woman's vocation to be mother." Quoted in Coriden, *Sexism and Church Law,* 90.

Chapter 2: And There Was a Woman

1. It may be appropriate here to mention two kinds of sources which are fundamental to this book: (a) all the Christian women of many denominations who are my friends, colleagues, students, or who have spoken or written to me about their experiences as women in the Churches, and (b) the writings of feminists, mostly women whose names will reappear constantly in these pages.
2. Particularly helpful have been Elisabeth Schussler Fiorenza, Elisabeth Moltmann-Wendel, Leonard Swidler, Rachel Conrad Wahlberg, Elisabeth M. Tetlow, and Karl Hermann Schelkle.
3. Vatican II, *Dei Verbum,* 10.
4. Raymond E. Brown, *The Critical Meaning of the Bible* (Ramsey, N.J.: Paulist Press 1981), 23ff.
5. Catherine of Siena and Teresa of Avila became part of the magisterium by being proclaimed Doctors of the Church in 1970, but the ongoing task of authentic teaching in Roman Catholic teaching is confined to the ordained all-male hierarchy.
6. Elisabeth Moltmann-Wendel, *The Women around Jesus* (Philadelphia: SCM, Fortress Press, 1982), 4.
7. At least since the days of Chrysostom, Origen, and Bernard. See Karl Hermann Schelkle, *The Spirit and the Bride* (Collegeville, Minn.: The Liturgical Press, 1979), 150.
8. Particularly helpful for this section have been two male feminists, Karl Hermann Schelkle and Leonard Swidler, *Biblical Affirmations of Women* (Philadelphia: The Westminister Press, 1979).
9. The phrase comes from the title of the book by John Meagher, *The Gathering of the Ungifted* (Ramsey, N.J.: Paulist Press, 1975).
10. Fiorenza, *In Memory of Her,* 72f, 148f.
11. Luke 13:34.
12. John 19:26; John 2:2.
13. Raymond E. Brown, "Roles of Women in the Fourth Gospel," Walter J. Burghardt, ed., *Woman: New Dimensions* (Ramsey, N.J.: Paulist Press, 1977), 112–123.
14. See, for example, the statement of the Canadian Bishops, *Ethical Reflections on the Economic Crisis* (1983).
15. In the synagogues, as in the Temple, separate sections were designated for the women.
16. Numbers 15:32–36.
17. See Swidler, *Biblical Affirmations,* 261ff.
18. Moltmann-Wendel, *The Women around Jesus,* 25.
19. Moltmann-Wendel, *The Women around Jesus,* 15–48.

20. The phrase is Martin Luther's, Moltmann-Wendel, *The Women around Jesus*, 18.
21. Burghardt, *Woman: New Dimensions*, 117.
22. Moltmann-Wendel, *The Women around Jesus*, 26.
23. Moltmann-Wendel, *The Women around Jesus*, 28ff, for a discussion of Martha in Christian art.
24. Fiorenza, *In Memory of Her*, Introduction.
25. Fiorenza, *In Memory of Her*, xiii-xiv.
26. 1 Samuel 10:1ff; 2 Samuel 2:4, 5:3; 1 Kings 1:39.
27. Fiorenza, *In Memory of Her*, xiv.
28. See note 13 above.
29. See, for example, the prayer from the liturgy for the Spread of the Gospel, *Daily Missal* (Ottawa: Canadian Catholic Conference, 1976), 1277.
30. This gospel reading is, appropriately, one of the key texts in the Enlightenment period of the Rites of Christian Initiation of Adults.
31. *The Revised Standard Version*, from which we quote here, places the text as a footnote.
32. Rachel Conrad Wahlberg, *Jesus According to a Woman* (Ramsey, N.J.: Paulist Press, 1975), 15f.

Chapter 3: A Ruler over Many

1. Kristen Stendahl, *The Bible and the Role of Women* (Philadelphia: Fortress Press, 1966), 18ff.
2. Romans 16:2.
3. Acts 8:3 (Palestine); Acts 9:12, 22:4-5 (Syria).
4. Acts 2:17-18.
5. Galatians 3:27-29.
6. Galatians 4:1-6.
7. See the analysis of this crucial passage in Fiorenza, *In Memory of Her*, 250ff.
8. Acts 1:21.
9. 1 Corinthians 15:3-9; Galatians 1:11-17.
10. See Epilogue.
11. John 20:18.
12. "Commentary on the Gospel of John," 13:28-29. See Schelkle, *The Spirit and the Bride*. 150.
13. Hippolytus, "Commentary on the Song of Songs," 3:1-4, quoted in Schelkle, *The Spirit and the Bride*.
14. Augustine, "Homily, no. 132," quoted in Schelkle, *The Spirit and the Bride*.
15. Bernard of Clairvaux "Sermon on the Song of Songs," 75.8, quoted in Schelkle, *The Spirit and the Bride*.
16. Romans 16:1-2 (sister); Romans 16:3 (co-worker); Romans 16-12 (toilers).
17. Fiorenza, *In Memory of Her*, 175.
18. Colossians 4:15; Romans 16:3,5.
19. Acts 16:15, 19-40.
20. Acts 18:1-3, 18-19; Romans 16:3-5.
21. Romans 16:1-16.
22. Josephine Massyngberde Ford, "Biblical Material Relevant to the Ordination of Women", *Journal of Ecumenical Studies*, vol. 10, no. 4 (Fall 1973): 676f.
23. Acts 18:1-3.
24. Acts 18:24-26.
25. "Homily on the Letter to the Romans," quoted in Swidler, *Biblical Affirmations*, 298f.
26. 1 Corinthians 12:28; 1 Corinthians 14:1
27. 1 Corinthians 14:33-35.
28. Schelkle, *The Spirit and the Bride*, 162-164.
29. For a convenient listing of this literature, see Swidler, *Biblical Affirmations*, 317ff.

30. See the discussion in Rosemary Radford Ruether, *Sexism and God-Talk*, (Boston: Beacon Press, 1983), 194f.
31. Chapter 7 below.
32. Romans 16:1–2; Acts 6:1–6; Timothy 3:8–13.
33. 1 Timothy 3:8–13.
34. *Testamentum Domini*, 1.23.17
35. *Didascalia*, 9.
36. *Apostolic Constitutions*, 8.3, a fourth century document.
37. See, among others, J. Forget, articles on "Diaconesses" in *Dictionnaire de Theologie Catholique*, vol. 4 (1), 685–703.
38. Epiphanius, Haer. 79.3. See also Jerome, Letter 51. The Council of Chalcedon, Canon 15, set the age for the ordination of deaconesses at 40.
39. The Council of Epaon in 517 (canon 21) ruled that all "consecrated deaconesses" are to be cut off from the Church.

Chapter 4: I Am a Christian

1. See the discussion of Christian historiography in William A. Clebsch, *Christianity in European History* (New York: Oxford University Press, 1979), 6ff.
2. The most recent edition of the text is to be found in Patricia Wilson-Kastner, et al., eds., *A Lost Tradition: Women Writers of the Early Church* (Lanham, Md.: University Press of America, 1981), 1–32.
3. W. H. C. Frend, *The Early Church* (Philadelphia: Fortress Press, 1982), 79–80.
4. Wilson-Kastner, *Lost Tradition*, 3.
5. Wilson-Kastner, *Lost Tradition*, 3.
6. Wilson-Kastner, *Lost Tradition*, 3.
7. Wilson-Kastner, *Lost Tradition*, 5.
8. Wilson-Kastner, *Lost Tradition*, 10.
9. Wilson-Kastner, *Lost Tradition*, 15.
10. Wilson-Kastner, *Lost Tradition*, 16.
11. Wilson-Kastner, *Lost Tradition*, 18–21.
12. Wilson-Kastner, *Lost Tradition*, 6.
13. Such a conflict followed the persecution of Decius, 250–251. See Henry Chadwick, *The Early Church* (New York: Penguin Books, 1967), 118ff.
14. Wilson-Kastner, *Lost Tradition*, "Introduction," 4.
15. Juan Hernandez Pico, "Martyrdom Today in Latin America: Stumbling Block, Folly, and Power of God" in *Martyrdom Today, Concilium*, vol. 163 (New York: Seabury Press, March 1983) 37f.
16. Hernandez Pico, *Martyrdom Today*, 39.
17. J. N. D. Kelly, [Jerome:] *His Life, Writings and Controversies* (Westminister, Md.: Christian Classics, 1980).
18. Derwas J. Chitty, *The Desert a City* (Crestwood, N.Y.: St. Vladimirs, 1966).
19. The development can be seen, for example, in the letters of Basil. See Letters 199.8.
20. Macrina seems to have been the first of her family to embrace monasticism and to have been largely responsible for the rule of life which was later followed by the whole family. "The Life of St. Macrina" in *Ascetical Works: Fathers of the Church*, vol. 58 (1897): 487ff.
21. Quasten and Burqhardt, eds., *Letters of Saint Jerome*, vol. I (Ramsey, N.J.: Paulist Press, 1963), Letter 127.5.
22. St. Jerome, Letter 126.
23. Jerome often describes his desert experience. See letters 5, 14, and the famous letter to Eustochium, Letter 22.
24. St. Jerome, Letter 45.
25. St. Jerome, Letter 29.
26. St. Jerome, Letter 27.
27. St. Jerome, Letter 22.
28. St. Jerome, Letters 38, 39.

29. St. Jerome, Letter 45.
30. St. Jerome, Letter 108.
31. St. Jerome, Letter 108.
32. St. Jerome, Letter 108.
33. Rosemary Ruether and Eleanor McLaughlin, eds., "Mothers of the Church: Ascetical Women in the Late Patristic Age" in *Women of Spirit: Female Leadership in the Jewish and Christian Traditions* (New York: Simon and Schuster, 1979), 72–98.
34. St. Jerome, Letter 108.
35. St. Jerome, Letter 108.
36. St. Jerome, Letter 108.
37. St. Jerome, Letters 45, 39, 108.
38. Palladius, E. A. Budge, trans., *Lausiac History* (Willits, Calif.: Eastern Orthodox Books, 1977), 41.
39. St. Jerome, Letter 39.
40. St. Jerome, Letter 108.
41. St. Jerome, Letter 127.
42. St. Jerome, Letter 59.
43. St. Jerome, Letter 82.
44. St. Jerome, Letter 127.

Chapter 5: The Light Comes

1. Frierich Heer, *The Medieval World* (New York: New American Library, Mentor Books, 1961), 317.
2. Heer, *The Medieval World*, 309–323. See also Eleanor McLaughlin, "Women, Power and the Pursuit of Holiness in Medieval Christianity," Ruether and McLaughlin, *Women of Spirit*, 99–130.
3. Reuther and McLaughlin, *Women of Spirit*, 104. Also see Sister Albertus McGrath, *What a Modern Catholic Believes about Women* (Chicago: Thomas More Press, 1972), 49ff.
4. Eileen Power, *Medieval English Nunneries 1275–1535* (Cambridge, Mass.: Cambridge, 1922), 237ff.
5. McGrath, *Modern Catholic*, 56ff
6. I cannot now trace the source of this expression, but see the discussion of the arts of courtly love in Heer, *Medieval World*, 157–196.
7. Paul Johnson, *A History of Christianity* (New York: Penguin Books, 1976), 191ff.
8. McGrath, *Modern Catholic*, 61f.
9. In 1928, Boniface VIII published the Bull *Periculoso* in an attempt to impose cloister on all religous women. This bull was renewed by the Council of Trent.
10. See the discussion in Eleanor Commo McLaughlin, "Equality of Souls, Inequality of Sexes: Woman in Medieval Theology," Rosemary Ruether, ed., *Religion and Sexism* (New York: Simon & Schuster, 1974), 213–266.
11. The lives of some remarkable women saints and mystics illuminate the period—Hildegard of Bingen is one who has gripped the imagination of many today.
12. For a readable account of the period see William J. Bausch, *Pilgrim Church* (Mystic, Conn.: Twenty-Third Publications, 1981), 256ff.
13. The reality of the plague is realistically portrayed by Barbara W. Tuchman in *A Distant Mirror* (New York: Alfred A. Knopf, Inc., 1978), 96ff.
14. See Maurice Keen, *The Pelican History of Medieval Europe* (New York: Penguin Books, 1968), 244ff.
15. There is an abundance of material available on the life of Catherine. This account depends mainly on Raymond of Capua, translated by Conleth Kearns, O.P., *Saint Catherine of Siena* (Wilmington, Del.: Michael Glazier, 1980); see also Alice Curtayne, *Saint Catherine of Siena*, (Rockford, Ill.: TAN Books, 1980).
16. Carola Parks, "Social and Political Consciousness in the Letters of Catherine

of Siena," Matthew Fox, ed., *Women Spirituality: Historical Roots, Ecumenical Routes* (South Bend, Ind.: Fides/Claretian, 1979), 249-260.

17. Curtayne, *Catherine,* 47ff.
18. Though Raymond of Capua had been appointed her confessor by the master general of the Dominicans in 1374, it is often difficult to know who is guiding whom. In Letter 373, she writes to him: "I beg and implore you, my father and my son, . . . resolve to begin a new life for yourself like a man dead to all the pull of his sense-nature, fling yourself into the service of the bark of Holy Church." Kearns, *Catherine,* xviii.
19. Kearns, *Catherine,* Introduction.
20. Quoted in Curtayne, *Catherine,* 91.
21. See letters in Curtayne, *Catherine,* 92ff.
22. St. Catherine, Letter 291.
23. Curtayne, *Catherine* 101.
24. Curtayne, *Catherine,* 96.
25. Curtayne, *Catherine,* 110.
26. See details in Keen, *History of Europe,* 277ff.
27. Kearns, *Catherine,* par. 334.
28. See, for example, Curtayne, *Catherine,* 38ff, 52ff.
29. Fox, *Women Spirituality.*
30. Curtayne, *Catherine,* 84ff.
31. Curtayne, *Catherine,* 48.
32. Curtayne, *Catherine,* 119ff.
33. Odilio Rodriguez, "Saint Teresa of Jesus: First Woman Doctor of the Church" in *Spiritual Life,* vol. 16, no. 4 (Winter 1970): 213-225.
34. Rodriguez, *Spiritual Life,* (Winter 1970): 218.
35. Johnson, *History of Christianity,* 228f.
36. Marina Warner, *Joan of Arc: The Image of Female Herosim* (St. Paul, Minn.: Vintage Books, 1981), 123. This book is my main source for this account of the life of Joan of Arc.
37. Johnson, *History of Christianity,* 191-264.
38. Warner, *Joan of Arc.*
39. Warner, *Joan of Arc,* 119, 54.
40. Warner, *Joan of Arc,* 122.
41. See Warner, *Joan of Arc,* 132ff for a description of the cults of Margaret and Catherine.
42. Warner, *Joan of Arc,* 160, 169.
43. Warner, *Joan of Arc,* 90.
44. Warner, *Joan of Arc,* 125.
45. Warner, *Joan of Arc,* 127f.
46. Warner, *Joan of Arc,* 143ff.
47. Warner, *Joan of Arc,* 140-141.
48. Warner, *Joan of Arc,* 117ff.
49. Warner, *Joan of Arc,* 15-28.
50. Warner, *Joan of Arc,* 121, 63.
51. Warner, *Joan of Arc,* 264.

Chapter 6: Carry Little Lanterns

1. A new era was inaugurated not only by the religious turmoil of the ages, but also by the discovery of America and the invention of printing.
2. See especially Mother M. Margarita O'Connor, I.B.V.M., *That Incomparable Woman,* (Montreal: Palm Publishers 1962).
3. Father Stanislaus, *Life of the Viscountess de Bonnault D'Houet,* (London: Longmans, Green and Co., 1916).
4. Johnson. *History of Christianity,* 298ff.
5. Hubert Jedin, "Reformation and Counter-Reformation," from *History of the Church,* vol. 5 (New York: Seabury Press, 1980), 431ff. See also Immolata

Wetter, "Mary Ward's Apostolic Vocation," *The Way*, Supplement 17 (1972): 69ff.

6. Wetter, *The Way*, 74.
7. For a brief account of Jesuit beginnings, see Johnson, *History of Christianity*, 301f.
8. A good description of the period can be found in Owen Chadwick, "The Reformation," *Pelican History of the Church*, vol. 3 (New York: Penguin Books, 1972), 253ff.
9. Ruth P. Liebowitz, "Virgins in the Service of Christ: The Dispute over an Active Apostolate for Women during the Counter-Reformation," in Ruether and McLaughlin, *Women of Spirit*, 132–152.
10. O'Connor, *Incomparable Woman*, 10f.
11. Chadwick, *History of the Church*, 226f.
12. Joy was one of the outstanding characteristics of Mary's life. In another time of turmoil she writes to her sisters, "Be merry, for mirth at this time is next to grace." O'Connor, *Incomparable Woman*, 84.
13. O'Connor, *Incomparable Woman*, 48.
14. Liege 1617, Cologne 1619, Treves 1620. O'Connor, *Incomparable Woman*, 60.
15. O'Connor, *Incomparable Woman*, 55ff.
16. O'Connor, *Incomparable Woman*.
17. These same charges had followed Mary from the early days in St. Omer, O'Connor, *Incomparable Woman*, 33.
18. O'Connor, *Incomparable Woman*, 110.
19. O'Connor, *Incomparable Woman*, 120.
20. O'Connor, *Incomparable Woman*, 115.
21. O'Connor, *Incomparable Woman*, 145.
22. Wetter, *The Way*, 71.
23. See Ruether and McLaughlin, *Women in Spirit*, 132ff.
24. Wetter, *The Way*, 85.
25. O'Connor, *Incomparable Woman*, 64f.
26. O'Connor, *Incomparable Woman*, 64f.
27. Wetter, *The Way*, 91.
28. Wetter, *The Way*, 91.
29. Wetter, *The Way*, 91.
30. The community dates its foundation to 1820: it received papal approbation from Gregory XVI in 1837.
31. For a briefer account of the life of Marie Madeleine D'Houet, see Mary Campion McCarren, F.C.J., *Faithful Companion of Jesus* (London: Catholic Truth Society, 1981).
32. The *Life* by Father Stanislaus details the relationship of Marie Madaleine with a series of Jesuit spiritual directors. See, for example, 33ff.
33. McCarren, *Faithful Companion* 11f.
34. McCarren, *Faithful Companion*, 15f.
35. McCarren, *Faithful Companion*, 20.
36. McCarren, *Faithful Companion*, 32.
37. Stanislaus, *Life*, 192.
38. Stanislaus, *Life*, 199ff.
39. McCarren, *Faithful Companion*, 43.

Chapter 7: The Church Teaches

1. Scripture scholars usually distinguish between the letters from Paul's own hand (Thessalonians, Corinthians, Galatians, Philippians, Colossians, Philemon), and those from his followers (Ephesians, Hebrews, and the Pastorals).
2. Galatians 3: 27–28.
3. See above, chapter 3.
4. 1 Corinthians, chapters 7, 11, 14.

5. In general, Paul based his argumentation on the second creation story which described Adam as the "source" of Eve's life.
6. 1 Timothy 2:9–15.
7. 1 Corinthians 11:16.
8. See, for example, Colossians 3:18–25.
9. Genesis, chapters 2, 3.
10. Pius XII "Allocution to Newly-Weds," *Woman in Modern World*, 62–63.
11. 1 Corinthians 7:1.
12. John Chrysostom, the "golden-mouthed" preacher, lived from 347–407.
13. See the analysis of the patristic writings in Rosemary Radford Ruether, "Misogynism and Virginal Feminism in the Fathers of the Church," Reuther, *Religion and Sexism*, 150–183.
14. Thomas Aquinas, *Commentary on the Sentences*, 1.92.1, ad.1.
15. Thomas Aquinas, *Summa Theologica*, II.II, 26, 10.
16. Thomas Aquinas, *Commentary*, 1.92.1.
17. Thomas Aquinas, *Commentary*, 1.92.1.
18. Thomas Aquinas, *Supplement*, 64, 5.
19. Thomas Aquinas, *Commentary*, 1,93,4. ad.1.
20. See the brief to the second Vatican Council made by Gertrude Heinzelmann in *We Won't Keep Silence Any Longer*, 79–99.
21. Sr. Joan Chittister, *Women, Ministry and the Church* (Ramsey, NJ: Paulist Press, 1983), 6–7.
22. This section relies on the excellent work by Nadine Foley, O.P. "Woman in Vatican Documents 1960 to the Present" in James Coriden, ed. *Sexism and Church Law* (Ramsey, NJ: Paulist Press, 1977), 82–108.
23. Coriden, *Sexism*, 64–69.
24. Quoted in Mary Bader Papa, *Christian Feminism*, (South Bend, Ind.: Fides/Claretian, 1981), 55–56.
25. Bader Papa, *Feminism*, 61.
26. Bader Papa, *Feminism*, 61.
27. See, for example, *Women in the Labour Force: Basic Facts* in the series of fact sheets produced by the Women's Bureau, Ontario Ministry of Labour.
28. See John XXIII, *Pacem in Terris*, par. 41; Paul VI "The Role of Women in Contemporary Society" (December 1974); and Paul VI, *Humanae Vitae*, par. 2. See also Vatican II, *Gaudium et Spes*, par. 60.
29. Paul VI, "A Call to Action," par. 16.
30. Paul VI, "The Role of Women in Contemporary Society."
31. Paul VI, "Role of Women," and see also Vatican II, *Gaudium et Spes*, par. 52.
32. Paul VI, "Address to Italian Catholic Jurists," (December 1972).
33. See chapter 1, pages 4–5 and note 10, page 155.
34. Abbott, *Documents*, 733.
35. Vatican II, *Ministeria Quaedam*, par. 7.
36. Letty M. Russel, "Theological Aspects of Women and Men in Christian Communities," *Bulletin International, Femmes et Hommes dand l'Eglise*, no. 17 (April 1976): 7. Quoted in Coriden, *Sexism*, 104.
37. *Origins*, vol. 13, no. 14.
38. "Woman as Gift", *CRC Bulletin*, vol. 23, no. 3, page 5.
39. *Catholic Mind* (Sept. 1981): 9.
40. *Origins*, vol. 13, no. 19, pages 334–335.

Chapter 8: Woman Church Teaches

1. *America* (May 5, 1984). The speaker is Elizabeth Carroll, RSM, quoted by Maria Riley in "Women, Church, and Patriarchy."
2. *Women Moving Church* (Washington, D.C.: Center of Concern, 1982).
3. Rosemary Radford Ruether, *Sexism and God-Talk*, 12–46.
4. See the analysis of feminist theologies in Fiorenza, *In Memory of Her*, part I, 1–95.
5. Genesis 1:31.

6. Pius XII "Allocution," *Woman in Modern World*, 67.
7. Chittister, *Women Ministry*, 10–17.
8. "Paternalistic Religion as Experienced by Women", *Concilium*, vol. 143 (1981): 69–74.
9. "God the Father in the Bible and in the Experience of Jesus: The State of the Question," *Concilium*, vol. 143 (New York: Seabury Press 1981): 95–102.
10. *Origins*, vol. 9, no. 18 (1979): 285.
11. *Origins*, vol. 9, no. 18 (1979): 292.

Chapter 9: Pray, My Sisters and Brothers

1. Almost all theological colleges now admit women students and each year the numbers grow.
2. A recent study by the Canadian Bishops' Task Force on Women, though not in any sense a scientific survey, amply confirms this fact.
3. The most frequently repeated reason for not implementing the Rite is that the basic ingredients are not present in the parish—community, lay ministers, and a sense of mission.
4. *Catholic Mind* (Sept. 1981): 7f.
5. Chittister, *Women, Ministry*, 12.
6. Organizations such as *Canadian Catholics for Women's Ordination* provide many women with a forum for discussion and discernment of the issues, as well as a community of support and affirmation.
7. In a statement to some American bishops, December, 1983.
8. Bader Papa, *Christian Feminism*, 55–56.
9. Marie Marshall Fortune, *Sexual Violence: The Unmentionable Sin* (New York: Pilgrim Press, 1983), xi.
10. Marshall Fortune, *Sexual Violence*, xi.
11. Marshal Fortune, *Sexual Violence*, 14f.
12. Matthew 22:1–14.

Select Bibliography

Brown, Raymond E. *The Critical Meaning of the Bible.* Ramsey, NJ: Paulist Press, 1981.

Burghardt, Walter J., ed. *Woman: New Dimensions.* Ramsey, NJ: Paulist Press, 1975.

Carmody, Denise Lardner. *Feminism and Christianity: A Two-Way Reflection.* Nashville: Abingdon, 1982.

Chittister, Sr. Joan. *Women, Ministry and the Church.* Ramsey, NJ: Paulist Press, 1983.

Christ, Carol P. and Judith Plaskow. *Womanspirit Rising: A Feminist Reader in Religion.* New York: Harper and Row, 1979.

Coll, Regina, C.S.J., ed. *Women and Religion: A Reader for the Clergy.* Ramsey, NJ: Paulist Press, 1982.

Coriden, James, ed. *Sexism and Church Law.* Ramsey, NJ: Paulist Press, 1977.

Curtayne, Alice. *Saint Catherine of Siena.* Rockford IL: TAN Books, 1980.

Elizondo, Virgil and Norbert Greinacher, eds. *Women in a Men's Church* (Concilium, vol. 134). New York: Seabury Press, 1980.

Figes, Eva. *Patriarchal Attitudes.* Salem, NH: Virago, 1978.

Fischer, Clare Benedicks, et al. *Women in a Strange Land.* Philadelphia: Fortress Press, 1975.

Flannery, Austin, O.P. *Vatican Council II: The Conciliar and Post-Conciliar Documents.* Collegeville, MN: Liturgical Press, 1975.

Fortune, Marie Marshall. *Sexual Violence: The Unmentionable Sin.* New York: Pilgrim Press, 1983.

Kolbenschlag, Madonna. *Kiss Sleeping Beauty Good-Bye.* New York: Bantam Books, 1981.

Mangan, Celine, O.P. *Can We Still Call God "Father"?* Wilmington, DL: Michael Glazier, 1984.

McCarren, Mary Campion, F.C.J. *Faithful Companion of Jesus.* London: Catholic Truth Society, 1981.

O'Connor, Mother M. Margarita, I.B.V.M. *That Incomparable Woman.* Montreal: Palm Publishers, 1962.

Papa, Mary Bader. *Christian Feminism: Completing the Sub-Total Woman.* South Bend, IN: Fides/Claretian, 1981.

Ruether, Rosemary Radford. *Sexism and God Talk.* Boston: Beacon Press, 1983.

Ruether, Rosemary Radford, ed. *Religion and Sexism.* New York: Simon & Schuster, 1974.

Ruether, Rosemary Radford. *New Woman, New Earth.* New York: Seabury Press, 1975.

Russell, Letty M. *Human Liberation in a Feminist Perspective—A Theology.* Philadelphia: Westminister Press, 1974.

Schelkle, Karl Hermann. *The Spirit and the Bride: Woman in the Bible.* Collegeville, MN: Liturgical Press, 1979.

Schussler Fiorenza, Elisabeth. *In Memory of Her.* New York: Crossroads, 1983.

Solesmes, The Monks of. *The Woman in the Modern World.* Boston: Daughters of St. Paul, 1959.

Swidler, Arlene. *Woman in a Man's Church.* Ramsey, NJ: Paulist Press, 1972.

Swidler, Leonard. *Biblical Affirmations of Women.* Philadelphia: Westminister Press, 1979.

Swidler, Arlene and Leonard, eds. *Women Priests: A Catholic Commentary on the Vatican Declaration.* Ramsey, NJ: Paulist Press, 1977.

Wilson-Kastner, Patricia, et al. *A Lost Tradition: Women Writers in the Early Church.* Washington, DC: University Press of America, 1981.

Selected Readings

The following books are also available from the Religious Education Division of the Wm. C. Brown Company Publishers:

Who Is My Mother

Covering both historical and future devotion to Mary, this new book explores her role and influence in the lives of Catholics. Some of the points it discusses are Mary as a model for women and priests, images of Mary, Mary's place in life and prayer, and how to recover a renewed, scripturally based devotion. Written by Mary T. Malone. (#2019)

Saints Are People: Church History through the Saints

Following seven historical periods, this informative reference profiles the lives and works of 31 saints. It gives a biographical sketch of each saint, the significance of his or her work, and a short reflection on the traits the saint exemplified. Written by Rev. Alfred McBride, O.Praem. (#1785)

Imagine That!

This creative resource discusses imagination, emotions, and phantasies as contributors to awareness, decision making, and motivation. Also covered is the use of phantasies in spiritual direction.

Imagine That! also contains 15 presentations that engage participants in a phantasy and then ask for reflection, meaning, and insight resulting from it. The phantasies can be used by an individual or a group. The phantasies are divided into three sections: Exploring Yourself, Exploring Your Relationship, and Exploring the Terrain Around You.

Also available is a 60-minute video cassette which demonstrates and discusses using phantasies. Following that are two phantasies complete with visual reflection/prayer meditation. The video is presented by the program's author, Marlene Halpin, Dominican.

> #1812 Book
> Video Cassette:
> 1838 ¾" U-Matic
> 1839 ½" VHS
> 1840 ½" Beta I
> 1841 ½" Beta II/III

Puddles of Knowing

This delightful book deals with teaching children to pray contemplatively. It chronicles a year's work with children, teachers, and parents. It offers insights, discoveries, suggestions, and scripture related to the many ways prayer develops a relationship with God. Each chapter concludes with a summary benefitting not only children's praying, but adults' as well. Written by Marlene Halpin, Dominican. (#2003)

Christian Spirituality for the Eighties

Just released, this new resource presents four separate papers dealing with different facets and approaches of spiritual development. Authors are Claire Lowery (who is also the editor), Howard Grey, S.J., Rosemary Haughton, and Peggy Way. (#1940)

Shared Faith is for the single, the married, the divorced, the widowed, and the elderly. It provides the resources and experiential techniques that address adults as adults. Written by Mary Jo Tully, each book in the *Shared Faith* series includes a collection of resource readings for the participants. Following each reading are two or three questions that call for the reader's reflection and how the reading relates to his or her personal life.

Included in each *Shared Faith* book is a guide for the group facilitator. It provides a four-step session outline consisting of an activity focusing on some dimension of the topic, exploring, discussing, and reflecting on the topic; scriptural reading, and prayer. These session outlines include music suggestions and additional discussion starters.

The four books of the *Shared Faith* series are:

Blessed Be

Nine sessions in which the adults are urged to discuss the Beatitudes in light of their own experience and belief.

Readings include: Blessed Poverty, Blessed the Gentle, Happy the Mourner, The Hunger Within, Beyond the Law, and Blessed the Pure in Heart. (#1822)

Church: A Faith-Filled People

Ten sessions focusing on the Church as a community where adults share caring, loving, and belonging through God and each other.

Readings include: We Are a Community, Love Does Such Things for Us, With Thanks to the Father, Our Forgiving God, and One God in the Spirit. (#1823)

Psalms: Faith Songs for the Faith-Filled

Eight sessions for adults to increase their appreciation of the Psalms and the enrichment they bring to prayer.

Readings include: One with the Father, We Believe, Out of Nothing, Sing a Song of Freedom, and Ever Faithful. (#1824)

No Other God: A Spirituality of the Ten Commandments

Newest in the *Shared Faith* series, contains eight resource readings and sessions for reflection upon and study of the Commandments.

Readings include: I Am Lord, My Name is Holy, A Day in Honor of Yahweh, And the Two Shall Be As One, and Choose Life. (#1942)

In His Light

This readable and concise resource presents the basics of Catholic faith along with current thoughts and trends developing within the Church. Each chapter is preceded by an allegory (which are excellent for meditations) and the book concludes with an index of Catholic prayers and pratices. Written by Rev. William A. Anderson. (#1716)

Journeying in His Light

Recently published, this formation guide presents 35 topics and session outlines. Using chapters from *In His Light* as background, sessions begin with a series of scripture references and include questions for discussion and reflection. Space is provided for composing personal thoughts and prayers. Each session concludes with a simple prayer. Written by Rev. William A. Anderson. (#1858)

For further information, contact:

WM. C. BROWN COMPANY PUBLISHERS
Religious Education Division
P.O. Box 539; 2460 Kerper Blvd.
Dubuque, IA 52001
(319) 589–2833